An Historical Guide to Malmesbury

Charles Vernon

Malmesbury Civic Trust

ISBN 0 9536692 1 1

Published by

Malmesbury Civic Trust,
Chalcourt, Dark Lane, Malmesbury, Wilts, SN16 0BB

Printed by

Antony Rowe Limited
Bumper's Farm Industrial Estate, Chippenham, Wilts, SN14 6LH

The two jewels in Malmesbury's crown - in the background the Abbey with its west end still in disarray and the Market Cross. The decorations are for Queen Victoria's Golden Jubilee in 1887. This event was celebrated in grand style including a feast in Cross Hayes with several lines of tables up and down the square. Points of interest are from the left;

No. 1 High Street occupied by James Barnard (b1848), watchmaker, jeweller and silversmith. Barnard seems to have been here from the mid 1870s to around 1890. This shop remained a jewellers up to the 3rd quarter of the 20th Century.

The licensee of the Green Dragon at this time was George Garlick (b1843).

There is a gas lamp on a bracket attached to the Market Cross just to the left of the white cross. One of the first lamps in Malmesbury was put at the Market Cross in 1836 but its position changed from time to time. This was taken down and a tall post erected a few feet to the right during the 1890s but that was removed after the introduction of motor vehicles and replaced by another hanging lamp this time on No. 1 High Street illustrated on page 11.

Hidden just to the right of the Cross is the Prince & Princess Pub. William Brown (1810-1880) had been the licensee and after his death his widow Ann took over until Charles Luce turned the building into the hospital.

The two storey building on the right was built as a Reading Room but in 1887 was just the Friendly Sabbath School, one of 10 Sunday Schools in the town, until bought for the hospital in 1893.

Introduction

It is 5 years since my first effort at publishing – *Malmesbury Then and Now*. I was amazed that the 500 copies sold within 6 weeks and I still occasionally receive requests for it. There were a few mistakes in it and the production was poor. Therefore this is a 'proper' book and rather more research has gone into this work. But I am sure that there will still be errors which once again are all of my own making. Much of the material has been gleaned from other published sources. Fortunately there is a lot available and details are provided in the bibliography.

So many individuals in the town have provided help with information, photographs and other valuable artefacts. I have been privileged to borrow these for closer examination. I am so grateful to you all and in particular must mention our Chairman, Roger Griffin who has allowed me to use his valuable collection of postcards. Many photographs from the Civic Trust collection are published here for the first time. I have to thank my wife, Val for her great help. She played an important role in research and her editing smoothed off many rough edges to the text.

I must once again pay tribute to the person who started my enthusiasm for the history of Malmesbury – Mike Fenton, the author of *The Malmesbury Branch Line*. His book is vital for anyone interested in the town as it describes so much more than the railway, it gives an insight into a bygone age. I draw your attention to two other titles that should be easy to obtain either in the library or from the town's booksellers. These are the extract from Victoria County History, *A History of Malmesbury* the publication of which was part funded by the Old Corporation and Major-General Sir Richard Luce's *The History of the Abbey and Town of Malmesbury*.

This book is set out in the form of two walks around the town. I appreciate that there is too much text to read as you walk but I hope that this will provide an excuse for visitors to return and residents to view locations in a different light. Although I have tried to provide a good index, I also use square brackets in the text to show where you will find further information about an individual or institution. This is not a complete history, not all the town's institutions, companies and organisations are described, some premises and people with interesting tales to tell have been omitted.

Finally you may wonder why the sections in the Walks have been chosen – the reason is that Malmesbury is covered by 4 different Ordnance Survey maps in the scale that I have used!

Charles Vernon May 2005

History

Throughout its history Malmesbury has witnessed some remarkable episodes, most of which are described in the text. However as the book takes you on a virtual tour of the town some events unrelated to buildings are missed. Therefore I begin with some general information. There has been a settlement on the top of the hill in Malmesbury for at least 2,500 years and probably for much longer. Not much is known about the ancient history of the town – very little archaeology has been carried out because there has been limited modern development and the rich written records of the monastery were largely destroyed after the Dissolution. However in 2000 we were fortunate to obtain funding to repair the town walls on top of the escarpment to the east of the town centre. A dig was carried out as part of this work and this uncovered evidence of Iron Age defences (c500BC).

The modern town results from an Irish monk called Maildulph establishing a hermitage and school c642, which attracted Aldhelm, kinsman of King Ine of Wessex. He was a great preacher and scholar whose fame spread throughout Europe. Famous for riddles, he would charm travellers with sayings and songs drawing them into the churches he had built here. His burial in the Abbey brought many pilgrims to view the Holy Relics he collected. They hoped that his miracles would cure them of their afflictions. So from Saxon times we have been a centre for tourists.

King Alfred recaptured the town from the Vikings in 878 and fortified it. He is supposed to have granted the town a Charter in 880 which would make it England's oldest borough. Around this time Malmesbury was on the border between Wessex and Mercia. Abbots used this to their advantage by playing one king against the other and in the process added great wealth to the monastery.

Alfred's grandson, King Athelstan further enhanced the town's position, making it his capital, holding court here and being buried in the Abbey. He was the first King of all England and gave King's Heath to the townspeople. The Abbey was still the economic base of the town and being so prestigious attracted considerable talent. Two notable monks were Eilmer and William. Eilmer around 1010 made the first flight by attaching wings to himself and flying from the Abbey. William of Malmesbury created a great library in the Abbey and wrote important histories of Britain. In Eilmer's time St. Aldhelm came to the rescue of the town. A party of Danes arrived to loot but one individual about to disturb the Saint's tomb fell dead whereupon the rest fled.

When the Normans took over the country Malmesbury was one of the most significant towns in England. In the Wiltshire section of Domesday it is the first listed, implying it was the most important. During the following century another anecdote confirms its status. In the 1140s Henry of Anjou took over the struggle to overthrow Stephen as King of England and Duke of Normandy that his mother, the Empress Matilda, had begun in 1139. In January 1153 he came to England with a very small army. He had support in the South West and quickly moved directly to Malmesbury. Using ladders his men scaled the wall and broke into the town. Priests and monks were slaughtered for which some mercenaries were dismissed. Henry besieged the keep of the castle but the castellan, Jordan, was able to summon help from Stephen. The king arrived with his army and arrayed it to the north inviting battle. However there was heavy rain and his troops were unable to cross the swollen river. He decided to return to London but before doing so agreed a truce which required him to destroy the castle. However after Stephen left Jordan simply surrendered it. This was a turning point in the war and later that year a treaty was signed whereby Henry would succeed Stephen.

At the Dissolution of the monasteries in 1539 the wealth of the monastery was lost. However it was not as important to the town as it had been and there were only a few monks remaining. In fact Malmesbury seems to have gained from the change, being able to benefit from a boom in the woollen industry with many empty buildings in which to manufacture cloth utilising the abundant water power around the town. This process saved our treasured Abbey church. During the 17th Century civil war Malmesbury changed hands no less than six times with the King almost captured here when he wished to stay overnight. At the end of the war Parliament ordered that the town walls be destroyed.

Unfortunately the woollen trade was cyclical and as it went into recession Malmesbury's influence declined. With a settled political system there was no need for inland defensive sites and other towns were better placed for trade. Major routes of roads, canals and railways missed the town and although a railway branch line opened in 1877, the age of Victorian expansion passed it by. This lack of disturbance and isolation has helped to preserve the town with a high number of listed buildings.

Malmesbury is now a prosperous centre of commerce. Dyson Appliances, manufacturer of vacuum cleaners and washing machines has its award winning futuristic headquarters at the top of Tetbury Hill. Much has been reported about James Dyson removing his manufacturing to the Far East. What the Press does not say is that Dyson's research and development is done in Malmesbury, as well as being hosts to the service and call centres. At the time of writing the Cowbridge House industrial estate is vacant and could provide further employment opportunities.

I end this section with a quotation from the first President of the Malmesbury Civic Trust which is a superb description of our wonderful town. I hope that I can illustrate some of these treasures with my words and pictures.

Malmesbury is a hill town of great and intimate beauty, clustering around its Benedictine Abbey, whose porch is like a via Romanesque manuscript rendered into stone. It is a place to walk about in once you have climbed the slopes, as all medieval towns were. But Malmesbury is lucky in having been built of the local limestone and in being a place for affording numerous vistas of Abbey and Tudor Market Cross, houses, cottages and chapels and every now and then between them there are glimpses of green hunting country and winding water below. By a miracle the town has escaped the self-consciousness of 'tourist beauty spots'. It has been little harmed by garish developments. This is a perfect English medieval limestone town, set on a hill welcoming all to nestle in its token shelter.

John Betjeman 1974

Contents

Walk 1 Station Yard to the Abbey

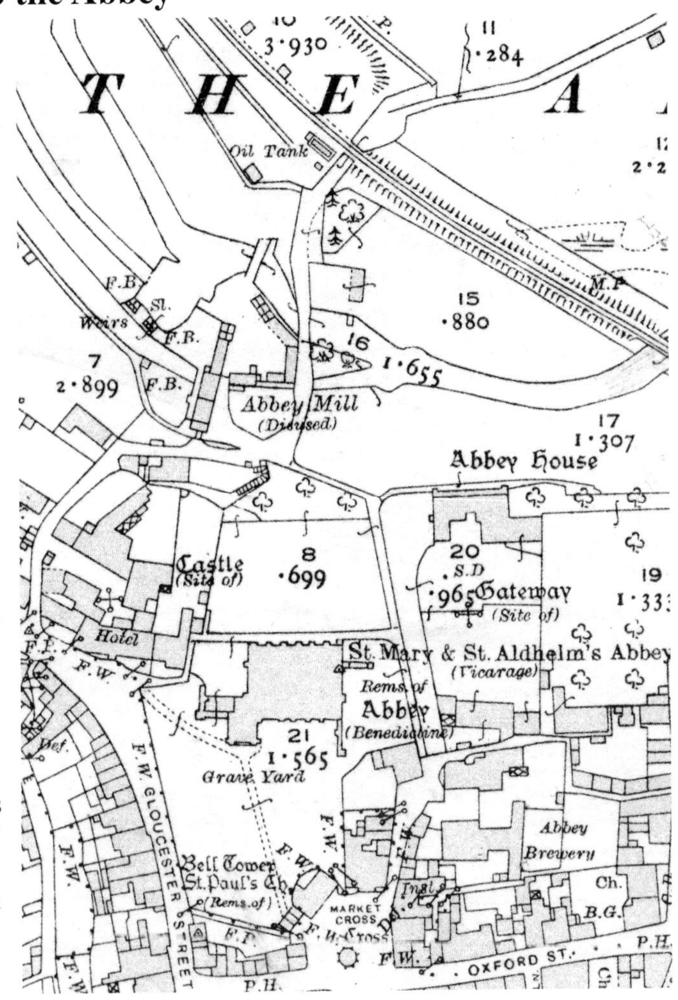

All of the maps are Ordnance Survey 1:2500 1921 Edition. At this time the Saxon central street layout was unaltered and many of the buildings described in the text are shown. However large areas of present day housing to the north and west like Parklands, White Lion Park and Reeds Farm were still fields.

The long stay car park and industrial estate has been built on the old railway. You will see that two streams that used to run where the picnic area now stands have been infilled. Cloister Garden (the rectangular area with 699 in the centre) was Abbey House's vegetable garden. Now their garden extends north of the river.

It is curious that the Cottage Hospital (just above the words Market Cross) is not identified, although the Maternity Home has Inst written across it. Just east of the Abbey Grave Yard is where the Athelstan Cinema was built in 1933.

We start at the long stay car park which was the site of the Railway Station until the 1960s.

Station Yard

Malmesbury was ignored by the early pioneers of the railway age. The first scheme seems to have been the Wilts & Gloucester Junction Railway of 1845. This would have connected Stonehouse with Chippenham via Tetbury and Malmesbury. Although some surveying was done it failed in the face of opposition from landowners. A number of other ideas were floated but few got very far until the Wilts & Gloucestershire Railway was considered. This intended to put a line from Christian Malford to Stroud. A great party was held on 1st July 1865 in a field near the Duke of York pub when the Countess of Suffolk cut the first sod. A very ornate spade and wheelbarrow used at this event can be seen in the Athelstan Museum (Town Hall). The jollification was premature as the problems faced by this Company could not be overcome and it was wound up in 1871. However land must have been purchased for this scheme as the development of the supermarket on the western side of Gloucester Road was held up in the 1980s when it was found that British Rail owned the land where the Railway Hotel stood.

The worthies of Malmesbury were not put off by this expensive failure and began discussions with the Great Western Railway, which the intended branch line of the Malmesbury Railway Company would join. In October 1871 a meeting was held in the Town Hall chaired by Colonel Charles Miles of Burton Hill House. Opened by Mr. W.S. Jones of Jones & Forrester [59 High Street], solicitors, it was attended by Walter Powell MP along with many other gentlemen and traders of the town. The proposal was to run a branch line to join the main line at Dauntsey, just over 6 miles away and estimated to cost £60,000. It was hoped that this would boost trade by improving the town's market and providing cheaper coal as well as enabling goods to be easily transported to and from the town. The station was to be sited on the largest area of flat land available to the north of the Abbey. Many troubles had to be overcome before the grand opening on 17th December 1877 and the full story is told in Mike Fenton's book, *The Malmesbury Branch.*

Some changes occurred quickly in the local community and economy. Henry Long (1830-1902) who ran a daily omnibus from the Greyhound [Smoking Dog], which he owned, to Chippenham (journey time 1½ hours) sold his transport equipment within a month of the railway's opening. House prices rose. Malmesbury's market held on the 3rd Wednesday of the month prospered and in February 1878 saw its best attendance for

A view of the Railway Station taken about 1910 as the west end of the Abbey has been repaired. The photographer is above the cattle pens which were at the end of the line. The engine shed on the left is the only building that remains.

over 30 years. However this enthusiasm did not endure and by 1900 the market was not so brisk. But trade for the Silk factory [Avon Mill] as well as for Adye and Hinwood's bacon factory in Park Road improved. Railway excursions were a feature with extra trains run for the Flower Show held at Burton Hill House. Notwithstanding this activity receipts did not cover the running costs and the company was taken over by the Great Western Railway on 1st July 1880. The other main items conveyed were coal and agricultural goods inwards with farm produce and milk traffic outwards. Stan Hudson [12-18 High Street] could remember milk carts driven by farmers' sons racing neck and neck either to get to the station first or just to catch the milk train.

The start of the First World War saw increased traffic on the branch with troops mobilising, military stores moving, Belgian refugees arriving to stay at Charlton Park and later war casualties coming to the military hospital there. Towards the end of the war services had to be scaled down due mainly to the shortage of men, rolling stock and coal. With the war over things returned to normal with tourists coming on special excursion trains.

The GWR began local deliveries of goods from the station in 1923 using a horse and cart later replaced with motor vehicles. However competition for passengers increased with more motor buses and coaches. The milk traffic diminished and by 1938 had completely been lost to road transport. Cost cutting measures had to be introduced and in 1933 the branch was connected to the South Wales main line, which had opened in 1903, at Little Somerford and the stretch to Dauntsey was largely taken up. This reduced the length of track to 3½ miles.

1st September 1939 saw the first train of evacuees arrive in Malmesbury carrying 900 children from London and about 200 of them stayed in the town with the remainder sent to nearby villages. The timetable was immediately revised with fewer services. However traffic increased as RAF personnel moving to and from the airfield at Long Newnton used the branch, as did medical staff after a military hospital was again established at Charlton Park. Linolite [the Maltings] received and despatched the goods associated with their production of de-icing hose clips. Later in the war prisoners-of-war arrived for local camps.

After the war's end the Labour Government nationalised the railways on 1st January 1948. Despite this, closure of the branch was considered but there was strong opposition from local businesses including Linolite, Ekco [Cowbridge House] and A.B. Blanch & Co. who started manufacturing agricultural machinery at Crudwell in 1950. However passenger services were doomed, and the last train ran on 8th September 1951. Goods traffic continued until 1962 and the track was lifted the following year. The station site was sold to the Borough Council in 1967 and developed into the light industrial estate and car park of today. The only reminders left are the old engine shed, used by Ebley Tyres for storage, the bridge abutments two hundred yards from Mill Lane and the tunnel under Holloway which can be seen from the River Walk during the winter months after the trees have lost their leaves.

Just before you come to the eastern end of the car park on your left you will see:

Lux Traffic Controls Ltd., Gloucester Road Industrial Estate
The head office of this company occupies a small unit, which belies its importance. George Lux, an electrician, came to Tetbury from London during World War II. After the war his family moved to join him and he opened an electrical shop. A customer asked him to make a set of temporary traffic lights and this request gave his son Lawrence the idea for a new business. Lawrence decided to manufacture and at first to sell, later to hire out, sets of traffic lights to control traffic around roadworks. The business started in 1967 becoming a private company in 1973. To begin with things were not very sophisticated, some of the early control units were assembled by Boy Scouts during 'Bob a Job' week! However innovative ideas soon produced new equipment such as the first vehicle actuated system using microwave detectors and specialist trailers for their own use.

Having outgrown the Tetbury shop their head office moved to Malmesbury by the 1970s. The company is now the world's largest manufacturer and hirer of portable traffic signals. They operate a 24-hour control room that is able to deliver to site equipment from 49 depots throughout the country. In 1997 BT awarded them a nation-wide contract and they provide training for many organisations including several police forces.

Across the road to the north east through the gateway is:

Conygre Mead
The name Conygre Mead means rabbit field and this provided a source of meat for the monks of the Abbey. For its water the town had relied upon wells, many communal, and some springs. For example several families along Bristol Street relied upon a spring whose water was (and still is) piped through the stone wall opposite the Plough Inn [12 Foxley Road]. A good spring was found in Conygre Mead on meadow land owned by the Manor. The Malmesbury Waterworks Company Limited was formed on 9th September 1864 with the object of providing water supply to the town. Lord Northwick gave the Company a perpetual right to take this spring water which was piped to a pumping station in Holloway (there is a small garden there now) from whence it was pumped to the tower near Abbey House. This tank gave much trouble in later years. The pump was originally driven by a gas engine, later electric. Every morning and evening it was switched on to top up the tank. During the day men from Wessex Electricity would keep an eye on the marker on the tower to ensure that the tank did not completely empty. There was concern over the purity of the water supplied by the Company and the lack of pressure, particularly on Sundays. After an outbreak of typhoid in 1899 the Borough Council wanted to buy out the Company and after arbitration over the price, £6,540, was able to do so in 1902. At that time the maximum output was 220,000 gallons per day.

During the 1940s a new source of water was found [Park Road Industrial Estate] and the Borough used Conygre Mead as a rubbish tip for about 10 years in the 1960s. It was sold in 1972 with planning permission for 11 houses which fortunately did not go ahead. In 1992 Malmesbury River Valleys Trust was formed with the intention of purchasing Conygre Mead and preserving it as a public open space. The Trust was able to buy it for £25,000, which was given to them by the North Wilts District Council, the Civic Trust and many generous private donations with a contribution from the Preservation Trust. If you have the time it is a pleasant place for a walk.

As you walk towards the Abbey you cross the River Ingleburn which rises near Tetbury in Gloucestershire. It is also known as Newnton Brook and on Ordnance Survey maps is called Tetbury Avon. Changes to the mill and the construction of the railway led to the watercourse being altered in this area. Just over the bridge you will see the remains of the mill leet on your left and on the opposite side:

Abbey Mill

There has probably been a mill on this site since at least Domesday. Abbot Colerne rebuilt a mill here in the 13th Century. The present building dates from the 18th Century. The Clark family lived here from the late 19th Century and in the 1950s William 'Cracker' Clark had a menagerie of animals including a monkey and a pet fox. His paddock across the river now forms part of the car park.

The Abbey Mill in the early 20th Century viewed from the top of the Abbey Steps.

Mill Lane

At one time the main Bristol to Oxford road came down this route, presumably to avoid having to pay a toll to go through the town. The river was crossed by a ford roughly where the stone crossing is now. The river here was used for mass baptisms [Abbey Row Baptists' Chapel], the last of which was held at the beginning of the 20th Century.

The last mass baptism in the river below Abbey House

Crowds would watch from the hillside and would often be rowdy. On one such occasion the Minister declared *There will be no laughter in hell* which quelled the laughter and allowed the ceremony to carry on in silence!

Abbey Steps

These were renewed in 2000/1 as part of a series of Town Enhancements mainly funded by the Heritage Lottery Fund and North Wiltshire District Council. Brass plaques depicting important dates in the town's history are set into the landings and were sponsored by various local groups and Councils.

As you climb the steps on your left are Abbey House Gardens with the building in front of you obscured by the wall and trees.

Abbey House

This house was either built by William Stumpe [Abbey Church] or his son Sir James around 1550. It was built on the undercroft of the 13th Century Abbot's house. Windows that were part of the original building are visible from the north side at ground level. There was a French priest in the Stumpe household who was probably responsible for laying out the grounds and gardens. The porch bears the arms of Sir James and his wife Isabel Baynton. In the 17th Century a low eastern wing was built and a long two-storey range running south from the western corner. This is the only large house in town to have survived from the 16th Century.

Thomas Ivy (d1672) lived in the house during the middle of the 17th Century. He acquired his wealth working for the East India Company but on his return to this country found that his wife had died. In 1649 he married Theodosia Stepkin, a widow who had spurned a suitor favoured by her father after he had been sick in her lap following a bout of drinking. Both parties to the marriage felt wronged by the other and Thomas published a pamphlet *Alimony Arraigned.* It was said that *he was knighted after the King's return but merited a whipping rather*. The family coat of arms is still over the chimneypiece.

During the 18th & 19th Centuries the house was divided into separate apartments. Dr Jennings (1818-1900), the Borough's Receiving Officer, lived in the house from around 1850 for the rest of his life. After his death the whole house was bought by Mr. (later Captain of the Lanarkshire Yeomanry and Household Cavalry during WWI) Elliot Mackirdy Scott Mackirdy (1881-1938). The Drill Hall near the base of the Water Tower was pulled down. He enclosed the area of the cloister with iron railings and turned it into

A view of Abbey House and the Abbey from Lovers Lane with the railway in the foreground at the start of the 20th Century.

a kitchen garden as well as carrying out extensive modifications to the house. Harold Brakspear (1870-1934, an architect from Corsham who worked on most of the area's important historic buildings as well as others further afield such as Windsor Castle) superintended the works. This included the demolition of both extensions with the eastern one being replaced by a two-storey wing with attics similar to the original building. The cellar floor level was excavated by six feet to return it to the same level as in the 16th Century. The house was occupied by the Deaconess Community of St Andrew from 1968 to 1990 to whom ownership passed after the death of Lady Eva Scott MacKirdy (1883-1971), but is now owned by Ian and Barbara Pollard. They opened the gardens to the public in 1998 and these have proved to be a strong attraction for visitors, drawn perhaps not only by the flora but also the Naked Gardeners!

Passing the Garden of Remembrance at the ruined eastern end of the Abbey in front of you is:

St. Michael's House, 14 Market Cross
This is believed to have been the site of St. Michael's Chapel, one of the original monastery chapels built by Aldhelm. One of his first miracles occurred during its construction. Many expensive roof timbers were cut ready for use but one was too short. The craftsmen brought this to Aldhelm's attention and after he prayed it was found to fit. This church was burnt down twice and each time this rafter was the only roof timber to survive the destruction. The present building dates from 1796 and has been used as a school, a malt house, at the beginning of the 20th Century the XXX Inn and more recently

as offices. In 2003 it was refurbished and turned into a townhouse and flat with a cottage at the rear.

Immediately beyond St Michael's House through the gap on your left you can see:

Abbey Brewery, Market Cross

Presumably a brewery was originally here to serve the monastery. The present building dates from 1672 with a 19th Century façade and was restored by Malmesbury Preservation Trust in the late 1980s. The North elevation has two storeys, the overhanging first floor supported by five stone columns with slightly tapering shafts. The brewery, owned by J.S. Ady in 1845, was later taken over by Luce's [the Maltings]. When it had been used as a brewery, the Maltster would dry clothes overnight for 1d. Edgar Farrow (b1841), Luce Brewery's manager lived in Brewery House. When the business was sold to the Stroud Brewery they sold the House and used the old brewery as a Sales Office where the Manager, Mr. E. Marmont was liberal with his samples. Apparently ginger beer and lemonade were also stocked here. The Stroud Brewery closed its office in 1941 but continued to expand elsewhere. By 1928 it owned 420 pubs and merged with another company to form West Country Brewery in 1959 which was swallowed up by Whitbread in 1967.

The modern houses to the right are:

St. Michael's Court (Athelstan Cinema)

After the short-lived Monte Duck cinema [32 Cross Hayes] the next experience the town had of this modern phenomenon was when a travelling cinema came to town in 1927. Jack L. Mott (1900-1981), his step-father and mother Mr. & Mrs. Collins set up their portable wooden building in the old Unicorn Inn yard [92 High Street] just off the road near the South Gate (where the Town Forge now is). Power was initially provided by a Lincoln Imp steam engine operated by 2 of the town's part time firemen, George Vanstone who worked at Ratcliffe & Sons (Foundry Road) and Dick Bishop (b1889). The piano was played by Arthur Phelps. After mains electricity was

The Athelstan Cinema shortly before demolition. It has lost the elegant white render of former days. St Michael's House is to the right.

connected talkies were introduced and the name changed to the Malmesbury Electric Picturedrome. The business prospered but disaster struck on 15th September 1934 when during a severe thunderstorm the structure was hit by lightning. Mr. Mott quickly drew up plans for the first purpose built permanent cinema on the site now occupied by St. Michael's Court. The finance was provided by Councillor James Jones [17 High Street]. There was much opposition to this proposal particularly from the Abbey congregation but the vicar, Revd. James Deane was in favour and expressed his support in one of his sermons. Four cottages were pulled down and the new Athelstan Cinema opened in 1935. This had 333 seats and a panoramic screen was erected in 1955. Between 1983 and 1988 it doubled as a Bingo Hall. Other events such as Carnival Flitch Trials (a couple would agree not to quarrel for a year and the evidence would be heard at the trial to see if they deserved the flitch, a side of bacon) were held here in late 1930s. It finally closed in 1988 and was demolished in 1993.

During the construction of the present houses in 2003 an archaeological investigation was carried out here. This revealed a graveyard and 76 burials of men, women and children. These bodies were removed for analysis leaving many more in situ. It seems that in medieval times this area was used for graves of the townspeople. This is a puzzle as St. Paul's was the parish church then and this cemetery seems to have been well within the grounds of the monastery.

As you reach the Market Cross Abbeyfield House is to the left whilst on the right is:

Whole Hog, 8 Market Cross

Charles Luce [the Maltings] whose eldest son Edward died in 1887 from typhoid, obviously felt that medical services in the town could be improved and gave premises previously used for the Prince & Princess pub (1803-1885) north of the Market Cross to become a Cottage Hospital in 1889. This was owned by Charles as owner of Luce's Brewery. The new premises were valued at £1,200 and had five beds. The building was inadequate and Charles bought the Friendly Sabbath School on the corner (which prior to 1870 also served as a Reading Room). The new premises were transferred to 12 trustees. Evidently even this did not meet the requirements for its new use. It was re-built in 1896 and outfitted at a cost of £1,200, which was raised by public subscription. This new building had eight beds, three male, three female and two private as well as an operating theatre. In the first year 47 patients were treated.

It seems that the town's General Practitioners have always run the hospital with specialists being called in when necessary. The local landed gentry subscribed to the running of the hospital in the early years and could provide a 'letter of introduction' for any employee who needed treatment to exempt them from charges. In 1910 the Board of Guardians of the Workhouse were charged 7s. 6d. per week when one of their inmates had to be admitted to the Cottage Hospital. Rule 2 stated that "Patients of unsound mind, epilepsy, enteric, infectious and contagious or incurable disease shall NOT be admitted." The Countess of Suffolk provided premises for a Maternity wing of the Cottage Hospital

The Market Cross and to the right the buildings that became the Hospital. The left hand one was the Prince and Princess Pub which extended northwards and wrapped around the two storey Reading Room latterly used for a Sunday School.

in Cranmore House [Abbeyfield House] in 1892. By the end of WWI the hospital was too small. Although an annex containing seven beds had been added in 1920 larger premises were needed. More room was required for patients and since only the Matron could be accommodated, houses had to be rented for the other nurses. The trustees explored the possibility of extending the Market Cross premises but the cost, £7,000, and other problems such as the noise of motor traffic (even though straw was often laid on nearby roads to deaden the sound) caused them to abandon this idea. The hospital moved to its present site on the Chippenham Road at Burton Hill in 1925. The old building was used as a shop by Jones & Son [17 High St.], an office for the Gas Company between 1935 and 1964, a cafe and a restaurant before once again becoming a pub in 1991.

Abbeyfield House, (Cranmore House) Market Cross.

Originally the Maternity wing of the Hospital and later used by the YMCA this is now a valuable home for older people capable of looking after themselves but in need of some support. The Abbeyfield Society, which now runs about 1,000 homes in Britain, was formed in November 1956. Richard Carr-Gomm, an ex Coldstream Guards officer, after working as a home help opened his first home for four residents in 1955. Each resident has their own bedroom with their own furniture but share a lounge, a dining room for meals that are provided by the housekeeper, and laundry facilities. In the early 1980s Nora Darling put together a committee of prominent local citizens to raise funds to open a local Abbeyfield. In 1982 one was opened in Long Street, Tetbury. A few years later an opportunity arose to purchase Cranmore House and the team swung into action again.

The Malmesbury home took its first resident in November 1987. There are nine rooms for residents with a live-in housekeeper.

Market Cross

This area was part of the Abbey precinct and originally a graveyard (an excavation in 1993 discovered human remains from c1020). Over the years the townspeople encroached onto the area until during the 13th Century Abbot Colerne gave it to them. The market area was delineated by St Paul's Church to the north and the White Lion Inn to the south spilling over to the west and east. The buildings on the north side of Gloucester Street are from a later date.

The Cross is presumed to have been erected around 1490, paid for by locals. When John Leland (1506-1552, Henry VIII's antiquary) visited the town in 1542 he described it; *There is a right fair and costly piece of worke in the market-place, made al of stone, and curiusly voultid for poore market folks to stande dry when rayne cummith. There be 8 great pillars and 8 open arches, and the work is 8 square: one great pillar in the middle berith up the voulte*. It is one of the finest surviving examples. It has been repaired many times, including just before 1800 by the Earl of Suffolk, in 1883 when £140 was raised by public subscription, between 1909 and 1912 by the Borough at a cost of £700 and in 1950 for £909 18s. 7d. The last major work, mainly cleaning, was completed in 1991 at a cost of £53,000, a large part of which was an English Heritage grant and the rest was raised from donations. The donors' names are displayed on an illuminated manuscript in

The Market Cross around 1905. The Green Dragon is on the left, the Hospital to the right with St Michaels House behind it. Note the magnificent gas street lamp in the left foreground attached to No. 1 High Street that remained in use for another half century.

the Mayor's Parlour. However the base of central column is still worn away from thousands of bottoms sitting there! In 1995 a large sum, including £109,000 from North Wilts District Council and £5,000 from the County Council was used to re-pave the area around the cross.

During Victorian times the Cross was not treated very well. Richard Jefferies (1848-1887, a journalist and writer) reported in 1867 that: *The cross is now looked upon with very little veneration. Vehicles are run into it for a temporary shelter, and the pillars are covered with printed bills of different colours; men out of work and other idlers have their great rendezvous.*

Rajah Restaurant, 6 Market Cross
Originally an Abbey hospitium (guest house) in the grand days of the 14th Century it still contains an original stairway. It seems to have become a public house called the Green Dragon for centuries until 1922. This pub was reputed to sell only pints of beer, no halves. The last licensee, Robert Roper turned the premises into the Abbey Café. Later it was called the Apostle Spoon until closure in 1996. After being unoccupied for a period, the Rajah Indian Restaurant opened in 1998.

Go through the 18th Century Tolsey Gate into the Abbey precinct. The gateway used to be the town's lock-up with two cells.

Abbey Church of Saint Mary and Saint Aldhelm, Church of England
The great builder, Bishop Roger of Sarum probably planned the present building, the third Abbey Church, which dates from about 1150 and was consecrated in 1180. At that time the estates of the Abbey were huge and as such demanded a magnificent headquarters. Its architecture is typical of the late Norman period with large circular pillars, rounded archways over the windows and doors with pointed arches, a newer style, between the pillars of the nave. The main doorway is particularly fine. The Outer Archway is about 18 feet wide. The lower outer parts depict Virtues conquering Vices, with what are believed to be signs of the Zodiac and Labours of the Months shown on the inner two lower columns. Thirty-eight scenes from the Old and New Testaments adorn the upper semicircles of the arch. They begin at the innermost left arch with the Creation of Adam and end with Pentecost on the outer right arch. Inside the porch there is a vision of the Lord in Majesty over the doorway and carvings of six Apostles on each side.

A reconstruction of the Abbey in the 14th Century by R.E. Woodman.

Further work was completed during the 14th Century including the raising of the roof to replace the wooden timbers with stone vaulting, new windows and the addition of a spire. At the end of that century a square tower was built over the two western bays of the nave and shortly afterwards the parvise was added above the south porch. The building was very much bigger than at present. The central tall spire, apparently 45' higher than Salisbury's, had a wooden framework covered with lead. This spectacularly fell towards the end of the 15th Century, possibly 1479 (although Brakspear believed that this occurred around 1535). The cause is unknown but one theory is that it was struck by lightning and the discharge of energy in wet stonework at its base might have been similar to an explosion. The fall effectively demolished the eastern end and provided a source of stone for a number of buildings – many carved decorative stones can be seen in buildings all over town. As a result about two thirds of the Church was lost. Nothing was done to rebuild the lost parts other than to erect a 'temporary' wall (still there!) at the eastern end of the nave.

After the Dissolution in 1539, William Stumpe (c1490-1552) bought the Abbey and outbuildings for £1516 15s. 2½d., a huge sum in those days. He was born at North Nibley (near Wotton under Edge) where his father was a weaver who became a clothier and parish clerk. William started out as a weaver and it is not clear how he earned his fortune but by 1524 he was one of the four richest men in Malmesbury. His eldest son

The west end of the Abbey before rebuilding. The base of the gaslamp in the centre foreground is still there.

A view of the Abbey from the south before the early 20th Century restoration. One of the coal stovepipes is in the centre.

James married Bridget, daughter of Sir Edward Baynton. Baynton took over the Abbey in December 1539 on behalf of the King. William Stumpe acted as his deputy for those properties that he subsequently bought! Leland reported that *every corner of the vaste Houses of Office that belonged to T'Abbay be fulle of lumbes to weve clooth yn and this Stumpe entendith to make a strete or two for clothiers in the bak vacant ground of the Abbay that is within the towne Waulles.* This development never took place. Leland also said that the town was producing 3000 cloths per year. By this time St Paul's, the parish church, was in a very poor state and Stumpe gave the Abbey church to the town The licence to use it as a parish church was issued in 1541. St Paul's steeple is now used as the Abbey's bell-tower. Stumpe was a very important man in Wiltshire being one of perhaps a dozen gentlemen chosen to govern the county. On his death he owned a vast estate of properties from Tewkesbury in the north to Warminster in the south.

It is not known when the west Tower of the Abbey collapsed but it was probably unstable when built as the nave had not been designed to accommodate it. The addition of bells hung from it following the fall of the main spire would not have helped. This second calamity seems to have occurred in the first quarter of the 17th Century (although Brakspear thought it was some 50 years before). No attempt was made to repair it, instead the nave was shortened by two bays and another new wall erected. Part of the remains of the central Tower fell in 1660. 4 arches are shown on the 1648 bird's eye map (you can buy a copy of this in the Town Hall). John Aubrey (1626-97, an antiquarian brought up at Easton Piercy) noted that during celebrations to celebrate the King's restoration *were so many and so great vollies of shot, by the inhabitants of the Hundred, that the noise so shook the pillars of the Tower, that one pillar and the two parts above fell that night.* Starting in 1822 restoration was carried out including a new Gothic window in the west end, the floor was raised to cover the square bases of the pillars, the triforium arcade repaired and the high pews removed. Walter Powell MP [King's Nursery] paid for gas lighting to be installed in 1875. More work was carried out at the beginning of the 20th Century, as parts of the structure were dangerous. The Bishop of Bristol, Forrest Brown, took it upon himself to raise the necessary funds. Two ruined bays at the west end were repaired and covered with a timber roof. The spiral staircase was completed to the roof and the walkway on the roof made accessible. Begun in 1899 and completed in 1912 this work cost £4,850 and was overseen by Harold Brakspear. This was the first project that he had carried out on a major building and it established his reputation.

In July 1927 the Abbey was closed to allow further renovation which was again supervised by Mr. Brakspear. The gas lighting had blackened the stonework and scaffolding was erected inside the Abbey so that this could be scrubbed clean. Two large coal fired cauldrons either side of the nave consumed ½ ton of coal each Sunday (but seemed to make little difference to the temperature) were removed. The organ was moved from the west end to its present position. The floor was lowered and the pews replaced with seats. Major General Richard Luce broadcast an appeal for funds on the wireless, the very first time that this had been done. A £7,000 bequest, which enabled repairs to start, ran out (£14,000 was spent in all) before all the work could be completed. The 1928 Carnival was devoted to the restoration fund and the tradition of a Mile of Pennies seems to have started then. A service was held on 6th December 1928 to rehallow the Abbey. Repairs to the roof had to be started after a piece of plaster fell down in March 1934. Sir Harold (he was knighted after work at Windsor Castle in 1931) prepared the initial report but he died on 20 November 1934 and his son Oswald took over. The work costing about £1,000 was completed by the summer of 1936. Maintenance of this ancient building is continuous as well as being expensive and donations are gratefully received.

The Cloister Garden to the north was established in 1980, the 1100th anniversary of the town's Charter and opened by Princess Anne. Having been blessed with another large legacy, further works have been undertaken including the renewal of the internal and external lighting completed in 2003. A major project is also under discussion to provide a place for meetings, possibly a facility for refreshments, and toilets. Further information about the Abbey can be obtained from the Stewards in the Abbey and the guidebooks available there.

A few of many remarkable individuals associated with the Monastery and Abbey Church are:

Maildulph
It is supposed that Maildulph, an Irish monk, established a hermitage under the fortification called Bladon around 642. There are a whole variety of ways of spelling his name ranging from Mailduib to Maeldulf, some times without the 'l'. Spelling was not a strong suit of Old English and many documents were written in Latin offering variants in translation. The hermitage is believed to have been sited in Burnivale under the fortified site in Abbey Row. He started a school that developed a community around it to support the scholars. This eventually became the town whose name is thought to be derived from

his.

Saint Aldhelm (c639-709)
Aldhelm was sent to Malmesbury to study under Maildulph, after initially being educated at Canterbury under Hadrian who had recently arrived in the country to spread the teachings of the Roman Church. Aldhelm was related to King Ine of Wessex and proved to be a great scholar and remarkable preacher. He was appointed first Abbot of the Benedictine Monastery in 675. Next he travelled to Rome. His host, Pope Sergius was rumoured to be the father of a new born baby. Aldhelm, no doubt anxious to please, asked the infant if this allegation was true. The child, all but nine days old, replied in a clear voice that Sergius was holy and undefiled. This miracle established Aldhelm's reputation in the Church. Many other miracles were attributed to him. For example when returning from Rome he brought back a slab of marble. En route the animal carrying it, probably a camel, fell injuring itself and breaking the slab. After a prayer the animal was healed and the marble repaired although there was a vein in the stone where it had been broken. Whilst on his travels Aldhelm was given and also bought many holy relics which he brought back to Malmesbury. He also corresponded with the foremost universities of the time in Bonn, Cologne, Paris and Pisa. Journeys to any of these places were formidable undertakings and must have taken a considerable time. Due to his royal connections and the fact that the town stood near the border between Wessex and Mercia the monastery estates were vastly expanded mainly through gifts from the two kings. It became the most important Abbey in southern England. When Aldhelm died in 709 he was brought back for burial in Malmesbury. The town then became a centre for pilgrimage with many more miracles occurring both at his shrine and at milestones along the route that his body had taken from Doulting, Somerset. After Archbishop Lanfranc heard of the miraculous cure of a crippled boy named Folkwine in Malmesbury, Aldhelm was declared a Saint in 1080.

John Scotus
During King Alfred's reign between 871 and 901 John Scotus (actually Irish but at this period Irishmen were always referred to as Scots) a man of clear understanding and amazing eloquence came to teach at the monastery. He came here from the Court of King Charles the Bald of France and William of Malmesbury tells a tale about his time there: *He was seated one day opposite the king at another part of the table. As the cup went round and the dishes disappeared Charles, whose face was a little flushed with wine, seeing John do something which might offend French fastidiousness, chaffingly said, 'What is it that stands between a Sot and a Scot?' John threw back the insinuation on to its author by replying, 'The matter of a table only!'* He came to a curious end because he was stabbed to death by his students with their pens.

King Athelstan (c895-939)
Grandson of Alfred and eldest son of Edward the Elder, Athelstan became the first King of England. On his father's death he took the crown of Mercia. Within a fortnight his half-brother died allowing him to take over Wessex and in 927 he conquered the Viking

kingdom of York. Coins minted in Malmesbury proclaimed that Athelstan was ruler of all England. He generously donated more gifts to our Monastery (details are given in Major-General Sir Richard Luce's book, *The History of the Abbey and Town of Malmesbury*) and held court in Malmesbury. He had a residence here and it has been said that this was on the site of Kings House in Kings Wall. This seems improbable as this was outside the town's defences but maybe he felt his charisma was so great that he was safe anywhere. There were certainly large Royal palaces at Brokenborough and Cowage off Foxley Road a couple of miles to the west of Malmesbury. The tomb in the Abbey dates from around 1300 and it is not known if it ever contained his remains.

Eilmer (d1060)
Around 1010 this monk is said to have made the first flight. William of Malmesbury's *Gesta Regnum Anglorum* (The Deeds of the English Kings) translated by Professor Lynn White described it thus; *He had by some means, I scarcely know what, fastened wings to his hands and feet so that, mistaking fable for truth, he might fly like Daedalus and, collecting the breeze on the summit of a tower, he flew for more than the distance of a furlong. But, agitated by the violence of the wind and the swirling of the air, as well as by awareness of his rashness, he fell, broke his legs and was lame ever after. He himself used to say that the cause of his failure was his forgetting to put a tail on his back part.* However the Abbott forbade him from trying again and he lived to be an old man.

William of Malmesbury (c1095-c1143)
Little is known about William, most information comes from casual references to his own experiences in his writing. He certainly spent his early life in the town. His father was probably Norman and well to do, so he could afford books that assisted William's education. At an early age William entered the monastery and he was soon helping Godfrey of Jumièges (Abbot from 1081 to 1106) to improve the library. It was not long before he started writing his own works. Queen Mathilda, widow of William the Conqueror, charged the Malmesbury monastery with the production of a history of the Kings of England. This became William's *Gesta Regnum Anglorum*, for the compilation of which he had travelled the kingdom and was first published in 1125. The first edition of *Gesta Pontificum Anglorum*, the story of various Bishops, the fifth book of which covered the life of St Aldhelm was completed the same year.

William was particularly well read being familiar with over 400 works written by 200 authors, so no doubt the Library was well stocked when he became Librarian. Around 1129 he visited Glastonbury and wrote about local saints followed by the *Antiquity of Glastonbury*. In that same year he produced a summary of Roman imperial history. He revised *Gesta Regnum* after 1135 and then worked on its continuation, the *Historia Novella*. Although he was a prolific author few of his works still exist, the monastery library was largely destroyed at Dissolution. Towards the end of his life he became Precentor (a senior member in charge of music) of the Abbey, apparently having turned down the Abbacy. It is not known when he died but it is believed to have been shortly after the last recorded event he wrote about in 1142.

The Abbey to Cross Hayes

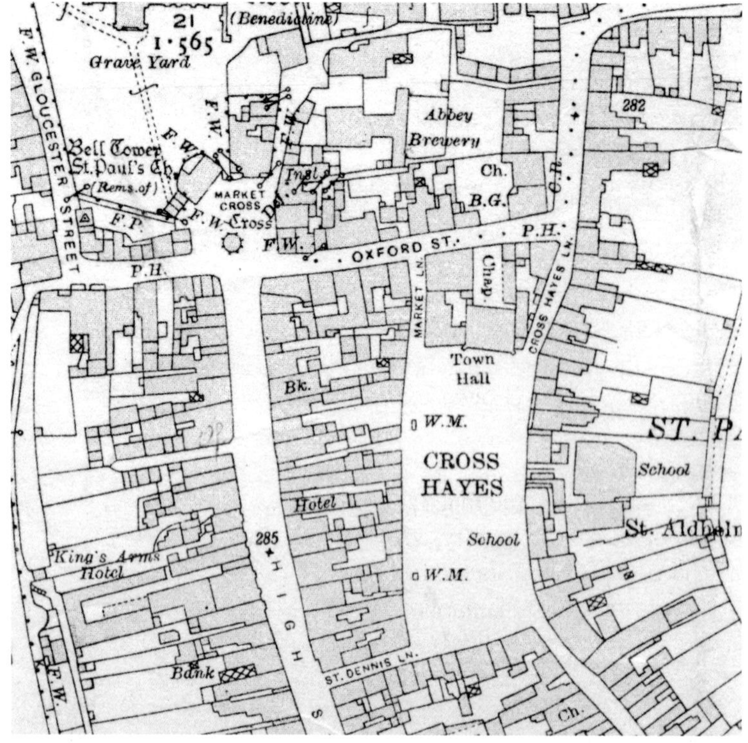

Not much has changed in the centre of town in the last 80 years. The 3 Horseshoes Inn (which had closed in 1921) on the corner of Oxford Street and Cross Hayes Lane was demolished in 1957 to widen the road. To the south of it a farriers abutted the Town Hall. There were 2 weighing machines in Cross Hayes for the cattle market. The Roman Catholic School in front of St. Aldhelm's Church has been demolished, the new school is in Holloway.

Retracing your steps back down the path you will see the belfry which was the spire of:

Saint Paul's Church

It is not known when this church was built. Certainly there was a St Paul's Church on this site during the late Saxon period. The last building here probably dates from the late 12th or 13th Centuries. The spire was built in the following century when some rebuilding was carried out. However by the time of the Dissolution the fabric was falling into disrepair and the nave was badly damaged by 1544. The Chancel at the east end was used as civic offices whilst the west tower was a private house. Later the area of the main body of the building, now called Birdcage Walk, was used as a lumber yard until all was finally demolished in 1852. The Chancel's south wall was reused as the back wall of buildings on the

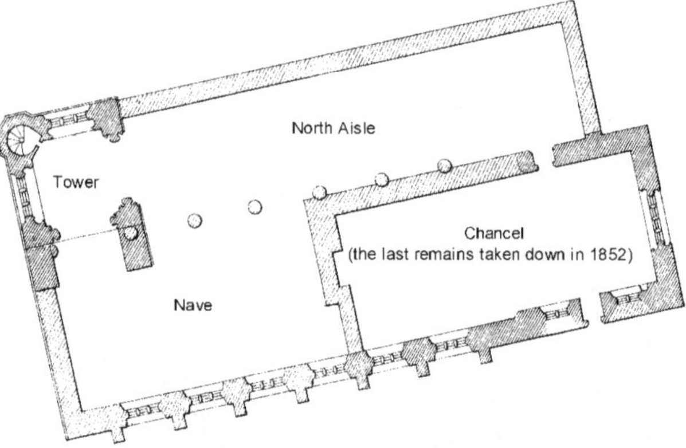

The plan of St. Paul's Church. The darker shaded areas are walls that have been incorporated into existing structures.

north side of Gloucester Street – you can still see the outline of windows and doorways.

The spire is used as the Abbey's belfry and when the Abbey was a separate parish it was unique that bells in one parish called worshippers to attend another! There are eight bells, the oldest of which is the treble inscribed *Sancte Georgei ora pro nobis* (Saint George, pray for us), however its exact age is unknown but may be earlier than the 16th Century. Two others date from the following century. One is supposed to have come from the Abbey. Whitechapel Bell Foundry carried out a major restoration in 1910. Malmesbury is fortunate in having an enthusiastic group of bellringers who raised a large sum of money in 1951 to purchase 3 new bells and retune the rest. The clock was made by Henry Weight in 1858 in his premises in what is now called Griffin Alley. A modern electric mechanism was added in 1952.

Cross the zebra crossing to the south side of Gloucester Street. To the right is:

8 Gloucester Street

This used to be the White Lion Inn with a name that apparently dates back to the 15th Century when the innkeeper, to demonstrate loyalty, adopted the Royal Crest of King Edward IV as his sign. It is said that the King stayed here before the battle of Tewkesbury. Richard Jefferies said the White Lion was *an inn of very antiquated appearance. The walls are said to be of immense thickness. It is considered to have been an appendage to the abbey, used as an hospitium, or place to entertain travellers, which*

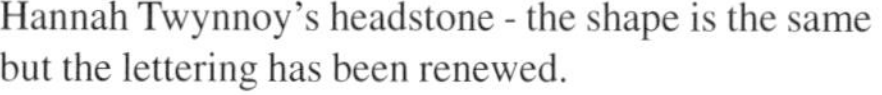
Hannah Twynnoy's headstone - the shape is the same but the lettering has been renewed.

The White Lion in 1964, before the bay widow was removed.

office it still fulfils. It probably dates back to the 12th Century. Its frontage would have opened on to the medieval market place and the rear courtyard extended to the town walls encompassing the present Gloucester House. This yard was used by a travelling circus during the early 18th Century. Hannah Twynnoy, a maid at the inn, teased the tiger, a very rare attraction at the time, that escaped its shackles and killed her. Her gravestone is in Abbey grounds, halfway between the Tolsey Gate and the main door. It is curious that a servant not only had a burial with expensive headstone in the Abbey but also a memorial in Hullavington church until renovations were carried out there in the 1870s. Clearly there is more to this story than we know.

In the middle of the 18th Century a Company of militia was formed in Malmesbury which met at the White Lion. The Improvement Commissioners [Gasworks] also held their meetings here from the end of that Century and continuing into the next. The Board of Guardians [Bremilham Terrace] held their first meeting here on 5th December 1835. At this time it was one of the town's coaching inns. During the run up to the Reform Act 1832 a banquet was held here for the non-reform party which led to a virtual riot outside. Before its closure in 1967 the inn was the oldest in town. Its bow window had a stained glass roundel with a white lion and the inscription 'Lord Mercy' which is now in the Athelstan Museum.

Turning left you will see the tower at the end of the street. Because of the narrow pavements it is best to walk to Market Lane and look back at:

Manor House, 6 Oxford Street

This building is thought to originate from about 1580. It is Grade II* listed and still has its original Elizabethan staircase. It is not clear why it is called the Manor House – before Dissolution the Lordship of the Manor belonged to the Abbey. The history of the Manor is difficult to follow (Luce has more details), most names of the Lords and dates of their Lordships are known but it was often sold, sometimes inherited and none of the incumbents seemed to live here. However in 1743 the Manor was bought by Sir John Rushout and thereafter it remained in his family.

The Manor owned much property around Malmesbury. This was either rented out or let on Copyhold. This curious form of ownership dated back to feudal times and was so called because a copy was made in the Court Roll. An annual rent was paid to the Lord and the land was let on the lives of 3 individuals who did not have to be in any way connected with the property or Copyholder. The copyholder would pick people with long life expectancy but also those whose deaths he would hear about - often members of the Royal family were named. On death a new life had to be added and a heriot or fine had to be paid to the Lord who could not prevent the nomination. If the holder failed to put in the new life a third party could do so and might eventually become the copyholder if he held all 3 lives. This type of ownership was abolished in 1922, but by that time the Manor had sold the freehold of all of the properties.

Oxford Street 1964. Kilmisters, cleaning & dyeing on the left with W. & E. Lockstone's next door. On the right is a hanging sign for Young, Sabey & Harris, electrical and radio engineers with 2 advertising signs, another sign for the Borough Arms and one for the YMCA. Note the roof on top of the tower in the background.

Messrs. W.&E. Lockstone bought the premises in 1808 and used them as a wholesale and retail grocer. They extended the front towards the road; you can see the shape of the original roof in the stonework on both gable ends. If you inspect the chimney stacks the stonework suggests that a roof was built against each gable, but roofs did not abut, the profile is the same on each end and is puzzling. At the rear, visible from the car park to Abbey Brewery, is an original window. Before the last war Lockstone's provided cigarettes as wholesalers to the workers constructing Hullavington aerodrome. Wartime rationing was based on pre-war usage and so Malmesbury never ran short of fags! The grocers shut in 1968 but it continues to be used as two retail units.

Guildhall Bar, 9 Oxford Street

In 1414 Henry IV gave permission for a merchant guild hall to be built. Monarchs strictly controlled places where large public gatherings could be held. The Guildhall Bar is probably this building. The oak roof has been dated circa 1420 and there is a rare late medieval pottery gable finial on the front of the gable end. Originally the hall would have been bigger, probably with five main roof trusses rather than the existing three. It was probably reduced in size around a century later and reconstructed with stone walls instead of oak columns infilled with wattle and daub. The outlines of doors and windows can be seen in the sidewall remaining from when the building comprised several cottages. Inside there are fireplaces high up the walls. The Old Corporation met here from 1414 to 1542. Refurbished in 1989 and used as the Old Guildhall Restaurant from 1991 to 1994, it then became a new pub, the freehold of which is still owned by the Old Corporation.

Wesleyan Chapel, 11 Oxford Street
John Wesley preached in the town three or four times between 1739 and 1741 but the Wesleyan Methodists first arrived in Malmesbury on Good Friday 1882 when they held an open-air service at the Market Cross. They sent a three-month mission that met in the Town Hall and services were held there until 1886 when the chapel was built. It had closed by 1919. The Wesleyans worked together with the Primitive Methodists for some time before merging with them in 1932.The premises were then used by the Young Men's Christian Association (YMCA) for about 50 years.

The YMCA first had a clubhouse in 1886 opposite the White Lion Inn in Gloucester Street. Around the turn of the century they moved to Cranmore House, Market Cross. During the First World War they moved again, this time to the old Wesleyan Chapel which was turned into a convalescent home for wounded soldiers. As soon as the war ended extensive building works started and in October 1920 Princess Helena Victoria opened the new premises. Snooker and billiards could be played on the ground floor with the upper floor being available for hire. The staircase was to the left of the doorway into the Club Room from Market Lane. The subscription was 10s. per year in the 1930s unless you lived more than 2 miles from Malmesbury when it was 4s. Presumably you were not expected to use the facilities so often if you lived out of town! In 1970 these premises were incorporated into the Town Hall. The club moved once more to Cranmore House for a few years before finally closing.

Moravian Church, Oxford Street
This denomination, the correct name of which is Unitas Fratum or Unity of Brethren, is the oldest free church in north Europe being founded in 1457. It was started by followers of the Bohemian priest, John Hus who was martyred in 1415. After years of persecution some of its members sought refuge in neighbouring countries, particularly Saxony though having come from Moravia that was the name by which they became known. In the 18th Century they became a Missionary Church concentrating on slaves in the West Indies.

John Cennick, who had been a Wesleyan evangelist and a follower of George Whitefield, started a religious society in Malmesbury during 1742. He invited the Moravian Brethren to take charge of congregations in North Wiltshire including Malmesbury in 1745. The Malmesbury society became a separate congregation in 1748. Cennick also began churches that he allied to the Plymouth Brethren and Baptists. However all of the North Wiltshire Moravian churches other than Malmesbury faded away after his death in 1755.

The chapel in Lower Oxford Street was built in 1770 and a schoolroom in 1860. The church closed in the mid 1990s and was sold. Services are now held in the church hall (the old schoolroom). After a couple of years anxiety whilst the fabric of the Church deteriorated, the owner has carried out extensive renovations.

The Society of Friends (Quakers) has had difficulty in gaining a foothold in the town although it had thrived in some nearby villages as well as Burton Hill. Towards the end of the 19th Century many members joined the Wesleyans and for a long time there was no group in Malmesbury. Joseph Cadbury had sought to revive the movement from 1894 but was unable to rekindle the flame in this area. In 1986 Arthur Minot started a meeting that is associated with the Gloucester and Nailsworth monthly meeting. Having met for some years at 22 Cross Hayes, a building then owned by the Church of England (the old Schoolmistress's house from 1857), since early 1999 they have used the Moravian Hall for their meetings.

Tower House, 13 Oxford Street

Although this has been a single dwelling since the 19th Century, it comprises a Medieval Hall with a Tudor rear wing and a terrace of 4 houses greatly altered during the 18th and 19th Centuries to the north with a 19th Century service wing. The site has a varied history. The earliest known use was as an Abbey hospitium (guest-house). The merchants' banqueting Hall, now the garage, was built around 1490. This has a 3-bay roof (formerly 4) with collar trusses and chamfered arch braces forming continuous arches, wind braces to the lower 2 registers and a through diagonal ridgc bcam.

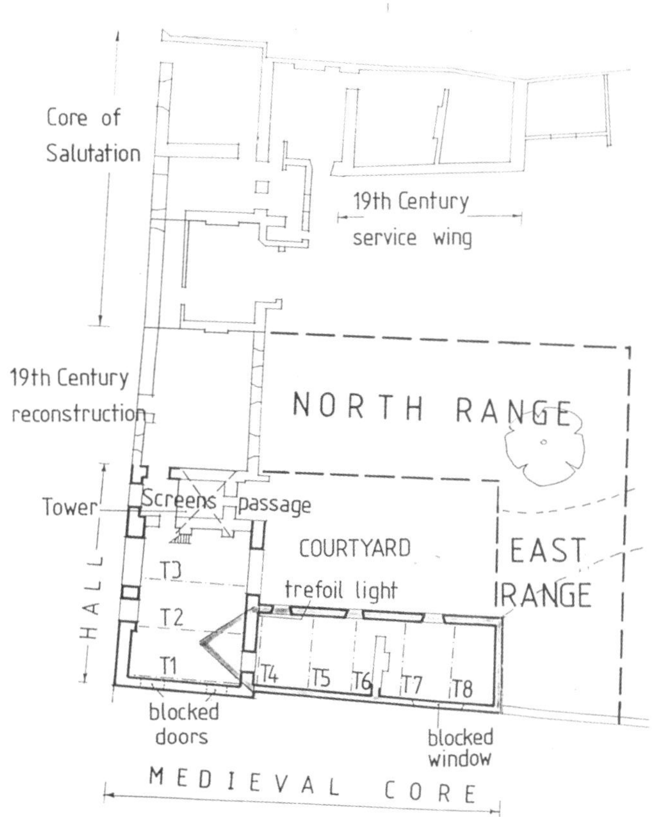

William Stumpe, the wealthy clothier who bought the Abbey at the Dissolution, lived in the Hall whilst building Abbey House. He built the southern rear wing for his home and stone from the Abbey was used in its construction, a trefoil window is an example. King Henry VIII after hunting in Braydon Forest arrived uninvited for a meal. Stumpe had apparently already eaten and had to use his employees' food for the King and his retinue. He must have looked after them well as he kept his head!

Charles I later stayed here during the Civil War. It is suggested that the parliamentarians set out to capture him but he was rescued in the nick of time by Prince Rupert coming from Cirencester. The 1647 'bird's-eye' map of the town shows an enclosed courtyard at the back of the Hall and a possible representation of this, prepared by David Stirling, North Wiltshire District Council's Conservation Officer, is reproduced. Robert Jenner may have built almshouses here in 1641 and probably these were the North and East Ranges shown on the plan. Part of these was demolished in 1825, the remainder later. A workhouse was established here from the 18th Century until 1838. It seems that this started in the Tudor wing (later the stables) but expanded to include the Hall, probably due to unemployment following the end of the Napoleonic War, problems in agriculture and the failure of Francis Hill's new factory at the Town Bridge. By 1838 a new work-house for 24 parishes around the town had been built on the Bristol Road.

Prior to 1803 the northern part of the terrace was a post house known as the Salutation Inn. Until recently there was a right of way from the garden of Tower House to Holloway, maybe allowing access for travellers with their horses to the rear courtyard of the inn. There is a basement and well under the present living room in the northern wing. Folklore suggests that a secret tunnel ran from there to Nuns Walk by the town wall but no trace of this has been found

The tower was added in 1834 by Dr. Player (1756-1864) for astronomy. This was built over the 4th bay of the old Hall. A gateway was made in the street side of the hall with a large opening on the east side to allow coaches to enter. It seems that the Handy family (lawyers who lived in Gloucester Street) owned the property from at least the early 19th Century although it was occupied by Dr. Alfred Jeston (1800-1869) after Player's death. Around this time it is likely that the doctor's surgery was established with its entrance underneath the tower. When Jeston died it was bought at auction in 1870 by William Thompson. By then all of the extensions to the northern part were complete. Dr. Richard Kinneir (b1842) started as Dr. Jeston's assistant but took over and finally bought the premises for £1,650 in 1897. Barbara Kinneir scratched her name on the glass of one of the bedroom windows.

The property was purchased by Arthur Heaton in 1919 whose widow sold it in 1929. Dr. Battersby ran the practice from then but after he was called out on a cold night he caught pneumonia and died. He was followed in 1938 by Dr. Willie Winch who is remembered for making his rounds in a 2 door open Bentley accompanied by his Siamese cat on the front seat! He was not particularly enamoured of the National Health Service and had many private patients. Despite this, having discovered a gravely ill farm worker he brought him back to health and he became the house's gardener. Dr. Winch moved and he used the house as a Nursing Home with staff living at Eastgate House two doors away. A number of rich eccentric residents were attracted by this facility including an ex

Indian Army Brigadier who would demand champagne and sandwiches during the night. Mentally ill patients could, as an alternative to being committed to an asylum, lodge with a General Practitioner and one such lady with her keeper resided here.

Observers photographed in 1940 by Edward Basevi.

Before World War II the tower became a post used by the Observer Corps. The Observer Corps was originally established in 1925. During the late 1930s it was greatly expanded along with other civil defence activities. In Malmesbury 6 part-timers were enrolled on 30 March 1939 in the Observer Corps of Special Constables. Whilst on duty they wore a blue and white brassard. During the war another 24 Observers were recruited. The Head Observer was Stan Hudson.

The tower of Tower House was designated as post M1, M2 was at Chippenham and M3 at Marshfield. Dr. Winch strongly objected to the disruption caused as access to the tower was originally through the house close to his bedroom. An electricity supply was installed (no doubt arranged by Ron Young of Wessex Electricity who was an Observer) and a canvas screen erected around the viewing platform. The first winter of the war was bitterly cold and a more permanent screen was built to protect the Observers. This was made of blocks with half of the platform open and the other half forming a covered shelter for 2 men. The Post Instrument was in the centre of the open viewing platform. This instrument was used to help determine the height, direction, speed and range of any aircraft seen. That information would be relayed by telephone through the Observer Corps 23 Group Operation Room in Bristol to the Filter Room at the RAF's Group 10 Headquarters, Rudloe Manor.

Complete and continuous observation was maintained throughout the war. Two Observers would be on duty at all times. No 1 was responsible for watching and listening for aircraft whilst the No 2 would identify them and report the information to Group using the telephone headset that he wore. He had to be proficient in aircraft recognition and was provided with silhouette drawings of many types of aircraft. To begin with the Corps did not provide training in this skill and it was only after individuals across the country started the Royal Observer Corps Club that it was taken seriously.

The police were at first responsible for the administration of the Corps but from 9 April 1941 it was reorganised, given the prefix Royal, new uniforms issued and the link with the police broken. The first uniforms were coveralls to wear over civilian clothes but during 1942 these were replaced by RAF style battle-dress. Nationally during the war there were 39 Observer Corps Groups which each controlled 30-50 posts. There were about 34,000 personnel in all.

At the end of the war the Royal Observer Corps stood down but was reactivated in 1947. By the 1950s the emphasis was on preparing for nuclear war. The tower was renumbered M4. It along with other posts at Minety M1, Highworth M2 and Toothill (Swindon) M3 was directly linked to 3 Group Headquarters in Oxford. A new underground bunker was built in 1962 off the Swindon Road not far from Maunditts Park Farm. The tower was still used and personnel climbing the stairs early on weekend mornings would often disturb the occupants of the house. Following another reorganisation in 1968 and the end of the ROC's responsibility for plotting aircraft both Malmesbury sites were closed. The Head Observer of the time, Bert Vizor and his colleagues then operated from Kemble airfield (post J3, Group 3) and later South Cerney. The Corps was disbanded on 31 March 1992.

In the middle of the war the interior of the tower had been improved with the new access from the garage. The wartime shelter on the roof was retained until the ROC lease expired. Later the shelter was dismantled and the wall reduced in height. Also during the war a governess originally from Alsace Lorraine known as Fraulein (but after the war Mademoiselle!) Rauch used the stables for a small kindergarten. Later the school moved to bigger premises but she continued to live there with her son for about 10 years. Having no bathroom she had to come into the house to bathe.

Dr. Winch did not wish to have a partner and would employ doctors as associates to help with the residents. However he spent more and more time in Guernsey and first employed Dr. Michael Pym as a locum in the winter of 1955. Three years later whilst suffering from mumps he decided to retire and sold the house and practice to Dr. Pym for £5,000. As mortgages were not readily available Dr. Winch gave him an interest free loan.

There were still a number of private patients including the Earl of Suffolk who expected to be seen even when he arrived without notice. The practice was expanding and Dr. John Rycroft became a partner. Unfortunately there was insufficient room in the house to provide the better facilities that modern medicine required. Several redevelopment schemes were considered until in 1979 the practice moved to Laystalls (so called because it was that place where dung collected from the streets was kept), Cross Hayes (now occupied by the Investment Centre). Tower House was sold to finance the move and for a time the old surgery was used for an antiques business by Mrs. Fidler. In the late 1980s A. Nielson, who ran Athelstan Coaches, owned the house and ran a guest house. André Ptaszynski, the theatre impresario, lived here for a year until 1992 when it was sold again.

Until the 1990s Tower House was the last property in the town that paid a Quit Rent to

Jesus College, Oxford. This was a charge made to release the house owner from feudal duties but it is not clear how this connection arose.

From here go south towards the open area which is:

Cross Hayes

Although the area around the Market Cross was used during the Middle Ages this was the main livestock market from Saxon times until World War II. A Hurdle Store (between Nos 12 & 14 Cross Hayes Lane) housed the hurdles to pen the cattle and hooks used to attach them to the buildings can be seen in the wall of No 14. This large open space has been used for many other events including a huge dinner for Queen Victoria's Diamond Jubilee and a celebration for the return of the volunteers from the South African War in 1902.

With motor vehicles now such an important part of modern life it is difficult to fully appreciate this space due to the many cars parked here. Aerial photos in the 1930s show no more than a dozen cars here and the only time recently when this was replicated was when a Millennium Party was held here in 2000. 'Pay and Display' charges were introduced in 1996 to try and encourage people to park elsewhere if they want to stay longer than 2 hours.

Town Hall

When facing this building in the Cross Hayes the half on the right was built as the Market House by the Malmesbury Market House Company in 1846/7. It was rented out

A market at the end of the 19th Century in Cross Hayes. Duck's malthouse, to the left of the Town Hall was rebuilt in 1927. The hurdles to pen the animals were kept in the Hurdle Store at the entrance to the square in Cross Hayes Lane. Hooks used to secure them can be seen in the wall of No. 14 Cross Hayes Lane.

Cross Hayes 100 years ago. The wall in front of the National School has since been removed together with much of St. Joseph's School next to it. Car parking spaces were marked out in the 1920s.

to auctioneers and by the end of the Century the lessees were Fielder and Rich. This firm was founded in 1795 and its successor, Fielder and Jones, still have offices at 10 Oxford Street. The building was described in *The Builder* of 29th July 1848 as follows; *Its chief front which faces the old cattle market in Cross Hayes consists of three arches with gates opening on to an area for pitching corn and cheese; behind are butter and poultry and other market places. Above is a large assembly room, roofed with timber, besides two smaller apartments. The front of the building is faced with carved freestone.*

It was called the Town Hall long before the Borough Council bought it in 1920 for £1,250 with £100 legal costs. Repairs such as a new hot water system came to an additional £903 18s. 11d. Councillor James Jones was largely instrumental in arranging this purchase and the subsequent enlargement of the premises. This was achieved by buying part of the adjoining building (on the left) in 1926 and rebuilding it. Originally there was a wool warehouse here but in the 19th Century it became the malthouse of Smith's Brewery taken over by Thomas Luce and then bought by Esau Duck in 1889. This property cost £300 and rebuilding amounted to another £2,598. Further expansion was completed in 1970 when the old chapel at the back on Oxford Street and offices on the Market Lane frontage were bought and a service core added to join the three separate buildings. On the reorganisation of local government North Wiltshire District Council took over the complex in 1974. Major refurbishment is now required to bring the structure up to modern standards.

Malmesbury Town Council is the successor to centuries of municipal governance but has little of the power formerly exercised here. The town is proud to boast that it is England's oldest Borough although regrettably there is no direct evidence to support this. It is said that King Alfred gave the town its first Charter in 880 but this is based on the

1381 Charter, the Saxon parts of which modern scholars feel are spurious. The Old Corporation [Old Courthouse] was replaced by a democratic Borough Council in 1886. C.R. Luce was appointed the first Mayor. The Council's area was larger than that controlled by the Old Corporation as it used the same boundaries as the Urban Sanitary Authority. In the south and east the rivers formed the boundary, from the Duke of York it followed the warditch on top of the Worthies to Stainsbridge, back down the river to Stainsbridge House, up Shipton Hill, cut across to Burnham Road, down Gastons Road to rejoin the river at Trucklebridge. The area was extended first in 1934, then in 1956 with the large area out to the bypass, Filands and Park Lane being added in 1984. Joseph Poole was elected Mayor in 1890. On relinquishing his office he donated street name-plates, some of which can still be seen today inscribed "Jos^h^ Poole ^Esq^ Mayor 1890-91". The Council comprised the Mayor and four Aldermen elected by Councillors for one and six years respectively and 12 Councillors elected by voters for three years. The Borough Council was the most important arm of local government until 1974 when most of its powers were passed to North Wiltshire District Council. The present Council has 16 members elected every four years and has the powers of a Parish Council. As had become normal on Local Government reorganisation (for the details see the Old Corporation) Malmesbury led the fight to be known as a Town rather than Parish Council. The Town Council now looks after a number of recreation grounds, administers the cemetery which is jointly owned with Malmesbury St. Paul Without Parish, manages the Town Hall on behalf of the District Council and provides information services for tourists and the general public from our larger hinterland.

For many years the Town Hall was used for dispensing justice locally. Before the last war sittings of magistrates were held on the first and third Wednesday of the month. From 1st April 1977 the Malmesbury magistrates ceased to be a separate Division but fortnightly hearings continued in the Town Hall until 1991. Although some local worthies continued as magistrates their administrative base was in Chippenham. The hearings were held in the Oxford or Hobbes Room and when the Athelstan Players were holding a production there the justices would appear amongst the scenery! The County Court, serving 43 parishes including Tetbury, also sat in the Town Hall from at least 1859. A century later Malmesbury was part of the Swindon County Court, but hearings were still held here monthly. Forrester and Forrester acted as Clerks to this court, but during the 1970s these hearings came to an end.

The Mayor, James Jones appealed in the Wiltshire Gazette of 19th February 1931 for exhibits for a new collection to be called the Athelstan Museum. At first this was housed in the Town Hall. In 1973 it moved to 20 Gloucester Street but the floor of those premises could not bear the weight of the proposed displays. On 24th April 1975 it reopened in the Town Hall. The museum is the responsibility of North Wiltshire District Council but at the time of writing they hope to transfer ownership to a local trust.

The Cross Hayes Infants and Girls Elementary School soon after it was taken over by the County Council around 1910.

Library

The 'National Society for Promoting the Education of the Poor in the Principles of the Established Church' after its formation in 1811 established a boys' school in the Guildhall, Oxford Street by about 1820. This was popular and on 2nd February 1857 two new schools were opened, one for boys in Gastons Road and the other for girls here. This school was built thanks to the munificence of Samuel Brooke and his nephew Revd. Charles Kemble and could accommodate 300 pupils. Children between 5 and 14 were offered education but the parents had to pay for it. Advance payments of 2s. per quarter were levied on poor parents and 10s. for the better off. No 22 Cross Hayes was the home of the schoolmistress and S.B. Brooke's arms are over the door. The girls were taught reading, writing, arithmetic and needlework. Older children could be employed as Monitors to supervise the younger ones and would receive a salary of £6 a year.

Government grants were available after the passage of the Education Act 1870. Unfortunately Revd. Kemble was unable to accept that Act's Conscience Clause which allowed parents to withdraw their children from religious studies. The school had some support from the Poor Law Guardians. After Kemble's death in 1875 the school was able to benefit from the government money. In 1964 the opportunity was taken to move this school into the old site of the Grammar School, Tetbury Hill.

Wiltshire County Council first provided a library in the town during the 1920s which opened for two evenings each week. The late 1930s saw the library in the Town Hall but from about 1940 to 1953 it operated from separate premises on the corner of Oxford Street and Cross Hayes Lane (this was demolished when the road was widened in 1957). In 1953 it moved to 44 High Street where it stayed until the present premises were taken over in 1972.

Cross Hayes House, 28 Cross Hayes
This town house was built in 1728 with a foundation stone on the south west corner inscribed WC 1728. It has a T plan with a projecting rear wing. In the late 18th Century an extension was added at the rear to the southeast. Charles Goddard Dewall inherited his uncle's estate [32 Cross Hayes] comprising a number of properties in the town. He was a Captain in the army and became ill whilst serving in Greece during 1856 with 91st Regiment. He went to convalesce in Italy and in his hotel met Father Marshall who had converted to Catholicism. Charles was similarly converted. On being posted to India he met Father Larive, a Frenchman, of the Order of St Francis de Sales. Charles had an ambition to reintroduce Roman Catholicism to Malmesbury (why is not clear – he was brought up in Corsham) and asked Father Larive to start a mission. Charles resigned his commission and the pair arrived in Malmesbury in May 1861. They intended to move into Cross Hayes House but unfortunately it had been let on a five-year lease which did not expire until 1866. Father Larive left to start a mission in Devizes whilst Charles became a Jesuit brother. After Father Larive took possession of the house he was able to say the first Mass in Malmesbury since the Reformation on Palm Sunday, 14th April 1867 in the parlour. A congregation of 22 from local towns and villages was present. Later the house became a convent first for Sisters of Mercy from Bristol who taught at the school from 1870 to 1884. Then the Order of St Joseph of Annecy took charge of the school. The nuns had intended that this would be their first residence in Britain but due to the problems with the lease had opened a house in Devizes instead. The convent closed in 1990 and although the house is still owned by the Church it has been let out since then.

St Aldhelm's Church
The original church was built in 1867 along the pavement of Cross Hayes to the north of Cross Hayes House and only the southern part remains. Within a short time the congregation had grown and larger premises were needed. Funds were short and Father Larive travelled to France and Italy seeking more. He was granted an audience by Pope Pius IX who gave him 4,000 lire. The present building was completed in 1875 and could seat 120. Father Larive had started in 1867 an evening school for working class men. This proved so successful that his parishioners urged him to open a day school for children of parents who could not afford the fees of the National Schools. This, called St Joseph's, was established in two rooms in Cross Hayes House the following year. When the new church opened they moved into the old building, able to accommodate 100 children. In 1932/3 new premises, costing around £6,000, were built in Holloway where there used to be a kitchen garden owned by the Kings Arms. It continues to be very successful and an extension was added in 1960.

A 1906 postcard view of the interior of St. Aldhelm's Church

There was much hostility towards the church and school particularly from the large number of nonconformists in the town. Attempts were made to force the closure of the school. Parents were visited to try to persuade them to remove their children. Father Larive was injured by a stone thrown at him. This tension led to him being recalled to Annecy having laid strong foundations for the faith. A reminder of him can be found in the Lady Chapel – a statue of Our Lady of Salette which he brought from France in 1866. He was succeeded by Father Decompoix who was priest for more than forty years. The numbers attending the church remained small until Father Morrin became the new priest in 1912. Energetically he became involved in the life of the community and made the doctrine of the church more widely known.

Father Morrin also raised money to improve the church. Just before the First World War a new sanctuary was built, heavy roman arches were replaced by slender gothic ones. Central heating and electric lighting were installed. The arrival of Father Grorod in 1925 heralded further work including a new altar and pulpit and the installation of three stained glass windows. These depict the Sacred Heart of Jesus, St. Mary and St. Aldhelm and were donated by the Bishop, having been removed from Bristol Pro Cathedral prior to its demolition. Father Grorod had served as an ordinary soldier in the French Foreign Legion during World War I. While saying his prayers in the barrack room he was interrupted by the rude remarks of his colleagues. Excusing himself to God he went and thumped the one making the loudest noise which enabled him henceforward to pray in peace. After World War II the sacristy was built and the old school demolished. In the mid 1960s, rose beds in front of the church were replaced by tarmac for parking and railings put on top of the wall next to the pavement.

32 Cross Hayes

This is a late 18th Century town house of two storeys with dormers and cellars. Mary Dewall a native of Purton, widow of Charles who died in Jamaica, bought the property for herself, her two daughters and a son, Timothy. Timothy became a doctor who practised in the town. In 1787 he moved to Burton Hill House and apparently rebuilt No. 32. On his death five years later he was in debt and was buried in the Abbey churchyard at night to avoid the attentions of creditors. His estate was left to his widow, Elizabeth and his sister Mary. They had to sell Burton Hill House and return here. Timothy had at least six children and his eldest son, Charles who was vicar of the Abbey in 1817/8 inherited the estate of his mother. Mary left her interest in this house to her nephew, Thomas, a younger son of Timothy. By the time Charles died in 1826 he had accumulated much property including Wynyards Mill, the Black Horse Inn, various cottages, several miscellaneous pieces of land, Cross Hayes House and another house in Cross Hayes. All of this was left in trust to his second wife, Sarah and daughter, Jane for their lives and on the last death would pass to any child of Jane's or if she died without issue the first son of his brother Thomas. Jane died before her father and the nephew, Charles [Cross Hayes House] obviously did not get on with Charles' widow, Sarah and started an Act of Ejectment against her. This was settled before it came to trial at New Sarum Assizes on 8th July 1826 with Sarah paying a considerable sum to Charles.

Around 1870 the house was bought by Esau Duck (1828-1908). He was the son of a miller, born in Blackland near Calne. At the age of 16 he walked to Malmesbury looking

The south east corner of Cross Hayes in the early 1970s. The building in the centre, No. 34 was the bus shelter then. From 1840 until 1954 it was the Brewery Tap, run by the Garlick family. Since 1998 it has been Henry George Estate Agents.

for work. He found a job at Crabb Mill (near Southfield Farm beyond the sewage works). He was a resourceful young man and eventually took over the business. Through his milling he accumulated wealth enabling him to move into this prestigious address in the centre of town. When the new railway line was being built Esau saw the opportunity to brew his own beer and sell it to the navvies. So he built a brewery behind his house and sold his produce for 1d. a pint. Later he bought the malt house at the top of Cross Hayes from Charles Luce. To finance this he went into partnership with his son-in-law Thomas Reed and the business became Duck & Reed. In the early 1880s Esau moved to the Beeches, Burton Hill and the Reeds lived at No. 32 until 1911 when they moved to Swindon. The firm was renamed Duck & Company. After Esau's death his eldest son Harry (1876-1950) became the brewer and after the Reeds left lived here. However the bulk of the estate valued at £72,000 (a fortune then) was inherited by the younger son Arthur Monte Jacob Duck (1888-1975) who had no interest in brewing and sold to Stroud Brewery in 1922. They wanted the 22 tied houses and Monte kept the old brewery building in Silver Street which he turned into Malmesbury's first picture theatre.

The town's first experience of moving pictures was in 1918 when a cinema van had visited the town to show views of the war following a lecture in Cross Hayes. Duck's new premises opened in November 1919. The shows were accompanied by Mr. Phelps on the piano – he later played for Jack Mott's cinema behind 92 High Street. Youngsters could attend a Saturday matinee for 3d. At this time films were often shown as serials with the last show on Saturday night depicting the hero (or more likely heroine) left helpless in dire straits until the next week's episode. Monte then had to rewind the reels and drive them to Kemble station for dispatch to the next cinema in the circuit.

By 1920 32 Cross Hayes was rented by Henry Beak (1865-1936) who ran Rich & Beak wine and beer merchants at 45 High Street, a business that closed in the 1980s. Later Henry bought the house and it remained in his family for around 50 years. The old brewery was used as a Drill Hall for a detachment of the 4th Wiltshire Regiment (TA) in the 1930s. After the war Athelstan Coaches had a garage there. More recently John Kadwell ran an antiques business from there until the premises was converted into prestigious offices and a flat in the new millennium.

Silver Street to St John's Bridge

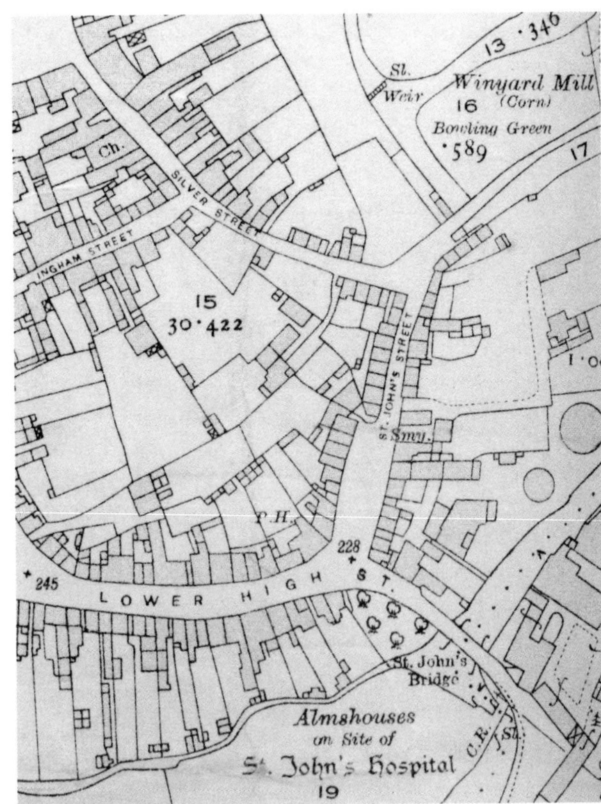

Several cottages have been combined to make larger dwellings. A row of cottages has been built south of the junction of Ingram and Silver Streets whilst another has been demolished in St. John's Street opposite Back Hill. Other demolitions include a large building in the Gasworks, the gasometers and a building adjoining the Old Courthouse which has been replaced by a number of garages.A small gasholder to the south west was removed between 1900 and 1920. The Bowling Green near Wynyard Mill replaced one which was north of Holloway at the beginning of the 19th Century. This green was made by the Malmesbury Bowls and Croquet Club formed in 1908. There were 4 rinks and a croquet green (for ladies) to the west, where 589 is written. The croquet green was lower than the rest and unfenced which created problems for the unwary in floods. The present clubhouse was opened in 1964.

Take the road south from Cross Hayes next to No. 32.

Silver Street

This is named after a mint operating here from the mid 10th Century for two hundred years. Unfortunately the exact site has not been determined. The Borough paid 100s. per year for the right to produce coins and this was the most important mint in Wessex. Coins minted here can be seen in the Museum.

King's Nursery, 4 Silver Street

Walter Powell MP (1842-1881) originally built this as Free Reading Rooms in 1870. Walter was the youngest of the three sons of Thomas Powell who owned coalmines near Newport and had interests in railways and shipping. Walter attended Rugby School between 1858 and 1861. His father died in 1863 and the businesses were sold. However the company Powell Duffryn stills bears his name. In 1867 Walter moved to North Wiltshire with his mother and rented Dauntsey House. There he made friends with the rector of Little Somerford, Rev. Arthur Evans. Evans was chairman of the Conservative Association and in December 1868 Walter was chosen as the Tory candidate for the

Malmesbury constituency. Early the following year he was elected as MP by 607 votes to 310 and ended 35 years of Liberal domination of the seat. A grand celebration was held for his supporters in the George Hotel in February 1869.

Tragedy struck his family that year when his eldest brother Thomas together with his wife and son were killed by outlaws whilst travelling in Abyssinia. Walter went to Egypt to deal with the formalities. On his return he started a number of works to benefit Malmesbury and the surrounding district. The first was the gift of these Reading Rooms. James Thomas Bird (b1839, a printer who lived in Abbey Row) in his 1876 *History of the Town of Malmesbury* described this as *a splendid building* (it would be cynical to suggest that his opinion might have been influenced just because Walter was his major financier!) and explained; *The first room is set apart for the use of the upper classes, and tradesmen, who choose to avail themselves of the privilege, and the inner room is provided for the lower classes. There is a large and capital Library, and a good supply of London and Provincial Newspapers, and Periodicals; all supplied gratis by the munificent donor of the building. The rooms are decorated with a fine collection of Buck and other horns, skins &c. Various games, such as Drafts, Dominoes, &c. are allowed to be played, the necessaries being also supplied by Mr. Powell.* The partition between the rooms could be removed to make a larger area for meetings. Four years later a games

Eclipse - the balloon in which Walter Powell made his demonstration flight from Cross Hayes.

room and soup kitchen were added.

Powell generously supported local social events and provided 50 tons of coal every winter for the aged poor of the town as well as giving tea and sugar. Residents of the Somerfords and Corston also benefited from similar gifts. He was an active supporter of the railway branch-line and provided gas lighting for the Abbey in 1875. Then he developed an interest in ballooning. In 1880 he met Henry Coxwell who took him on a flight. He was so taken with the pastime that he spent a lot of time pursuing it and in October of that year had to send a telegram to apologise when he was unable to propose the election of a new coroner. In June 1881 he wished to give a demonstration to his constituents. Thomas Wright brought his balloon, Eclipse, to Cross Hayes. This was inflated from a specially laid gas pipeline joined to a 4½" main in the High Street. The balloon apparently took 20 hours to fill and the town was without gas for the night! The day of the flight was treated as a local holiday with the Town Band and another from Didmarton playing. The flight itself was over within an hour, the balloon having travelled west over Lea and Somerford. He rented a field next to the gas works in Bath so that it was easy to make regular flights.

Walter became friendly with Captain James Templar of the balloon department at Woolwich. They had a spherical balloon of Lyons silk made up at the Silk Factory in Malmesbury and completed it at Powell's home in Somerford. The car was fitted with the latest improvements including cork seats and life belts. Unfortunately this was not used when Walter Powell made his last flight on 9th December 1881. He, Templar and Mr. A. Agg-Gardiner took off from Bath at 1.55pm in the Government balloon Saladin to make observations for the Meteorological Office. By 4.40pm they could see the sea near Bridport, Dorset and sought to land. Part of Templar's report reads; *I opened the valve and descended about 150 yards short of the cliff. The balloon, on touching the ground, dragged a few feet and I rolled out of the car with the valve line in my hand. This caused the balloon to ascend about 8 ft. when Mr. Gardiner dropped off and unfortunately broke his leg. I found that the rope was being pulled through my hands, and I called to Mr. Powell, who was standing in the car, to come down the line. He took hold of the line and in a few seconds it was torn through my hands. The balloon rose rapidly. Mr. Powell waved his hand to me. I took a compass bearing.* It was said that the balloon had fallen into the sea and with a reward on offer boats searched for several days. But it was not until 27th January 1883 that the Penny Illustrated was able to report that the balloon and car had been discovered in the mountains of the Sierra del Pedroso in northern Spain. Walter's body was never found and Malmesbury lost one of its greatest benefactors.

On 17th August 1882 4 Silver Street and other properties were auctioned by Walter's Executors and the Borough Council bought it for use as the Council Chamber. The particulars read; *All that substantial and well-built Messuage and Premises, Situate at Silver-street, Malmesbury, lately used as Reading Rooms, having a frontage of 24 feet, and running the total length of 170 feet to the rear of the premises. The rooms are lofty and well-ventilated, and divided by a pair of folding doors; gas and water laid on; has an excellent coal cellar, and underground passages. At the rear thereof is a capital Sitting-room, Kitchen with cooking range and offices. There is an excellent light and airy Bedroom above, and Water Closet on landing. The whole of the grates, chandeliers and other gas and water fittings will be included in the purchase.* Whilst owned by the Borough the premises were used as the Technical School [Malmesbury Secondary School] from its opening in 1892 to 1902. When the Council moved to the Town Hall the Bristol Diocesan Trust paid £500 in 1921 to use it as Parish Rooms. It became a schoolroom during World War II and in 1951 was sold to the Catholic Church.

The Kings Church took over the building in 1967. This is a Pentecostal church, the origins of which date back to 1948 when Mrs. Rowe of Swindon had a vision telling her to come to Malmesbury. Going down the hill from the Triangle she walked past St Mary's Lane but was guided back to the TocH Hall (now the small house called Westport Studio), which was next to St Mary's Church. Here the first meetings of the Assemblies of God Pentecostal were held. A few years later they moved into the Food Office (now the Council Chamber) in the Town Hall when rationing ended. The modern Pentecostal movement began in Los Angeles in 1906 with some extraordinary spiritual manifestations. The Reverend A.A. Boddy, an Anglican priest, introduced it shortly afterwards to Britain. The Assemblies of God were constituted in 1924, adopting a congregational form of government. The Kings Nursery now uses the Silver Street building and has proved so successful that the church has moved to the old Baptist chapel in Abbey Row.

Ebenezer Chapel, Silver Street

The Independent Church was formed in 1796 when services were held in a cottage in Berry's Entry, High Street (now No. 43). The premises were too small and two cottages for sale in Silver Street were converted into a Meeting House. The church united with Westport Presbyterians during the pastorage of Rev. Edwards who took up his post in 1812. The Chapel was sold and used for trade. In 1814 and again in 1825 Primitive Methodists from Sherston hired the building for a short time. This group received rough treatment from the locals who regarded them as 'ranters' who had no right to be treated with civility. Soon afterwards the Baptists moved in and held services here for over 10 years.

The Independent's union with the Presbyterians, although flourishing at first, failed to prosper as not all the congregation had consented to it. In 1841 Friends of the Old Independent took over the building. The premises were enlarged in 1848. More work was carried out in 1885 including the removal of the old pews and the installation of bench seating for 300 at a cost of £300. An adjacent cottage to the south was converted into two classrooms. In 1914 there was no settled minister and it was again proposed to reunite with Westport Congregationalists. The deacons resisted this and for a time it would seem that the church prospered as the building was refurbished during the late 1920s. At this time Sydney Adye of the High Street grocers was the treasurer. It was not until December 1952 that finally the two churches permanently united. The building has been used as the Masonic Lodge since 1958.

Freemasons - St Aldhelm Lodge No. 2888

This, one of the largest lodges in Wiltshire, had its origins at an informal meeting at the Bell Hotel in 1900. Joe Moore, the Bell's proprietor and Baldemiro de Bertodano, a wealthy retired solicitor of Spanish descent who lived at Cowbridge House, decided to try and form a lodge in the town. At the beginning of 1901 a dozen prospective members agreed to petition for one. It was consecrated with a service in the Abbey in the summer of 1902.

After the end of World War I the Lodge was the only one in Wiltshire to become a 'Hall Stone' Lodge in recognition of the money it raised towards the new Masonic Hall in London intended as a Peace Memorial. Meetings continued at the Old Bell Hotel for many years until the end of World War II when the Town Hall became a temporary and inconvenient home. In 1958 the Freemasons moved to the Old Independent Church in Silver Street where considerable works have been carried out over the years. The Lodge is a very successful fundraiser for charities, having raised £25,000 in the late 1990s with a commitment to raise a similar sum in the first five years of the Millennium.

Walking south you will come to Back Steps at the site of the Little Gate – this is where the later Town Wall cut across the southern slope of the town. Earlier it had followed the line of Ingram Street. Until recently the cottage at the bottom of the steps was called 'Curfew' – a link to the past when the gates were closed at night. Behind a closer cottage to the west, standing on the Town Wall is:

Culver House, Culver Gardens, Ingram Street

This 16th Century house was divided into 3 in the middle of the 19th Century. Culver means dove or pigeon, which was used as a source of meat. The house is reputed to have been the residence of Parliamentary Military Governor Col. Nicholas Devereux, from 1644-6 and later the home of the notorious Dr. Edmund Wilkins (1726-1804). Alderman and from 1775 High Steward of the Old Corporation, Edmund was an apothecary. At first he was a supporter of Henry, 12th Earl of Suffolk who served as High Steward 1762-8. He then became Deputy High Steward to Charles James Fox and carried out many of Fox's duties. In 1775 he was elected High Steward and remained so until his death in 1804. He was the first Malmesbury resident to hold this post for over 100 years and when he took over the town had been solidly Whig since the beginning of the 18th Century. He controlled the election of the town's two MPs in the following manner. Ten of the thirteen electors (the Alderman and twelve Capital Burgesses) gave him a bond of £500 for which he then paid them an annuity of £30 (provided that they supported his candidates and annually re-elected him as High Steward). Towards the end of his life he had difficulty in making these payments and left £500 in his will to be distributed between the Capital Burgesses to clear the debt. He sold the Parliamentary seats to the highest bidder until 1789 after which he supported government candidates. In 1796 there was a contested election for the first time in half a century. The Whigs put forward Mr. Vassar as candidate. Although he had much support in the town he received only one vote. He petitioned Parliament to overrule the election but failed. Wilkins also was Receiver General or tax collector for the County and a magistrate

Wilkins held dinners for the Capital Burgesses which were always sumptuous affairs. At one of them he introduced the latest import, cigars. Unfortunately his guests did not know what to do with them – they saw Mr. Wilkins bite the end off his but he was then distracted and they continued to try to eat them! This amusing tale comes from a speech made by A. Fraser to the Malmesbury Literary and Debating Society long ago; *THE EFFECTS OF A GOOD DINNER, followed by trying to chew, and smoking cigars and drinking wine, this select company got right happy and jolly, and when they departed many had difficulty to get up and walk or get to the door, and when they got outside the fresh air had a most singular and strange effect on the feasters, for they began to go reeling round and round like spinning tops, knocking one another over. Also the cigar had the same result on their stomachs as it has on naughty boys when they have smoked their first pipe - it made them retch.*

Mr. Wilkins had a statue of St. Aldhelm, which formerly stood in the Abbey, erected on a pedestal in his garden. One of the Burgesses, endeavouring to go home, happened to wander off the path into the garden, and went up to where the statue stood and addressed it as follows:-"Bisent thee coming whoam?" Getting no reply he said "Don't stick up there like a dumel, you girt gawney you, come on" and suiting the action to the word he put his arm around it and gave a lurch, when both rolled over on to the ground together, where he went to sleep with his arm around the prostrate statue. Early next morning, Isaac Cook, Mr, Wilkins' groom, going through the garden with his lantern to the stables (which have since been converted into cottages), thought he heard someone snoring, and going across the garden to see who or what it was, found this worthy Burgess fast asleep by the side of the statue. Recognising him by the light of his lantern, he addressed him thus: "Jumes, what bist thee doing here, you drunken slipot?" (at the same time giving him sundry kicks to wake him). "Get up. Why, thee hast bin an' pulled St. Old 'un off his perch. Did'st thee thenk as how thee had'st the Missus alongside on 'e? Thee had'st better shamock off and make thyself scarce afore the Squire gets about, for 'e sets main store on thuck image as 'e used to be in the old Abbey," (and giving the sleeping Burgess more kicks,) "for if he finds thee here, Jumes, thee wotent find nothing under thee plate when thee dost come to supper next turn." "Thee bide a' quiet, Isaac," said Jumes, rubbing his eyes, "and doesn't thee let on to the Squire as how thee's found I here, for he 'ull send round for I to put the 'Saint' on his stand again - well, thur now, one job makes another - I'ull stand thee a quart of Saml. Hanks' 'stingo'" (his best beer) "when I sees thee round at The Bear." "Mind thee doesn't forget it then, Jumes," said Isaac, and with the light of his lantern turned on to the garden, old Isaac exclaimed, "My blessed, what a rucket! and what a feegarie all on 'em must have had last night - the husbirds (or whosbirds) - a scrambling and hocksing about - and the messes all over the pleace, for when I turns the dogs out they'ull find their own bre'kfusts, and

it'ull take I main of the mornin' to put it all in track agen. Bless my heart and soul if it won't," said Isaac, making his way to the stables.
It was said that hardly any of the Burgesses knew how they got to their homes from this banquet, and many were not seen for several days after. Also it was said for a fact that none of them brought away with them anything that was put on their plates, only that which they found under their plates! This is a reference to the Trinity Tuesday dinners when the annuities would be paid.

At the bottom of the steps you can take a quick diversion to stand on Goose Bridge and look at the steep escarpment with the recently repaired Town Wall at the top. At the end of the Civil War, Parliament ordered that the Town Wall be destroyed but here most of it survived because it held back the adjoining gardens! Return along St John's Street for 300 yards and on the left an archway leading to:

The Old Court House, St John's Street
The School Arch is so called because it led to the Old Corporation's School. This was held in the Old Courthouse which is on the left through the arch. The school was set up at the end of the 16th Century and was open to all sons of commoners. Under an agreement of 1609 the Corporation paid £10 a year for the master. After 1694 Michael Weekes added another £10 from land at Great Somerford. In 1714 the master was dismissed because he lived outside the town and appointed a deputy who presumably

The Old Courthouse in the 1950s. In recent times the Old Corporation has spent much money refurbishing its properties. The upper part of Culver House appears above the roofs.

was badly paid because he demanded fees from the pupils! The school closed in 1890 when the 20 scholars were transferred to the National School. The rent charge was paid to the National Society until free elementary education was introduced the following year.

The Courthouse probably dates from the 14th Century and is thought to be a remnant of the Hospital of St John the Baptist. However it originally extended further to the south. It is now the headquarters of the Old Corporation of Malmesbury. The origins of this body come from Anglo-Saxon times when King Edward the Elder confirmed the town's status as a Borough. The freemen of the town were granted five hides of land (about 600 acres – still known as King's Heath) by King Athelstan as a reward for their help in defeating the Danes at Brunanburh. This reputed Charter of 925 reads:
I Athelstan, King of the English, on behalf of myself and my successors grant to my Burgesses and to their successors of the burg of Meldufu that they may have and hold always all their tributes and free customs, as they held them in the time of King Edward my father, fully and in honour.
And I enjoin on all beneath my rule that they do no wrong to these Burgesses, and I order that they be free from claims and from payment of scot.
And I give and grant to them that royal heath-land of five hides of land near my vill of Norton, on account of their assistance in my struggle against the Danes.
The Charter of this grant has been confirmed by my seal by the witnessing of Edmund, my brother, and by the advice of master Wolsin my chancellor and Odo my treasurer and Godwyn.
Godwyn, who bears the King's standard, obtained this on behalf of the Burgesses.

It was not until 1635 when Charles I, having made an investigation into the governing bodies of boroughs, granted a further Charter which formerly recognised the Corporation of the Alderman, 12 Capital Burgesses and 24 Assistant Burgesses with a High Steward as advisor and man of law to be the body to administer local government here. These officials, other than the High Steward, were drawn from the commoners of the Borough. The commoners have four 'ranks' – commoner, landholder, Assistant Burgess and Capital Burgess. In modern times until the summer of 2000 membership was restricted to men who fulfilled the following requirements: he was a son or son-in-law of a commoner, was married and lived within 1½ miles of the centre of the Market Cross. On admission a new commoner is entered into the list of one of the six 'hundreds' – Taylors, Fishers, Glovers, Coxfoot, David's Loynes and Thornhill. Each of these has 31 members. The initiation ceremony, which used to take place at Kings Heath entailed firstly digging a shallow hole in the turf. Into this the prospective commoner would put a silver coin and the following would be said to him: *Turf and twig I give to thee, as King Athelstan gave to me, a good brother thou shalt be*. Then the initiate would be struck across the back three times with a twig. When a vacancy occurs in the hierarchy through death or discommoning the most senior commoner is promoted to the ranks of the landholders. Advancement above this is by election, an Assistant Burgess being elected by all the Burgesses and a Capital Burgess by the remaining survivors.

Until the start of the 18th Century any male inhabitant could be a commoner provided that he was married and occupied an ancient tenement in town. In 1727 new rules were introduced restricting commoners to those outlined above together with their apprentices (this last was removed in 1821). In the early 19th Century the commoners felt that they were not getting the full advantage from Kings Heath which was largely overgrown. An Act of Parliament was obtained in 1821 to allow the Heath to be split into allotments to allow each commoner to share in the cultivation of it. This Enclosure Act fixed the number of commoners at the number existing then, 280, each allocated around 1½ acres (those closest to town were smaller, the furthest ones larger). Unfortunately modern lifestyles have reduced the numbers that could meet the criteria and in 2000 there were only 216 commoners. Therefore the rules have been changed to include women and unmarried people who can show that they are descended from a commoner and live within the 1½ mile radius. This has filled the ranks once more.

Richard Jefferies had the following to say in 1867; *It is even said that the true Malmesbury population are all more or less intimately related – one great family. This is one advantage of a corporation – it makes men perhaps greater friends, more attached to their native place; and imbues them with what is called esprit de corps. At the same time it debars progress .Some even stigmatise the corporation as the ruin and bane of Malmesbury, asserting that there is not a single tradesman in the place who is really a Malmesbury man in proof of this statement. Such may now be the case, but it is evident that of yore the corporation has been of the greatest service to this town.* As you read my

The interior of the Old Courthouse in the 1920s. Apart from the gaslighting the photo could have been taken yesterday.

account you will find that nearly all of the entrepreneurs mentioned were 'incomers'.

The Old Corporation meet at four Courts which are held on Trinity Tuesday, King Athelstan's feast day (the following Tuesday), Michaelmas (29th September) and New Year's Eve. The land to which this body owes its origins, Kings Heath, still belongs to the Old Corporation 11 centuries after it was given to them. Due to the need to maximise food production, Kings Heath was taken over by the War Agricultural Committee in 1940 and the allotments disappeared. It was not until 1951 that control returned to the Old Corporation but with the proviso that it was to be farmed as a single entity.

The Alderman and Capital Burgesses were also responsible for electing Members of Parliament. Malmesbury was one of the true rotten boroughs - two MPs elected by thirteen voters. Before the Reform Bill the Malmesbury's MPs were Tories and none of the later members were associated with the town. Sir Charles Forbesse was reported in the Morning Chronicle of 17th May 1832 to be not prepared to pay as much to be the town's MP as previously, a sum supposed to have been 12,000 guineas. The Reform Bill of 1831 was hotly debated in the town. Under the Act the borough lost both MPs but a subsequent amendment reinstated one for a new constituency that included several nearby villages. Malmesbury was the only place where this happened. Ironically most of the old 13 electors were disenfranchised as they did not own their own property!

However the town was excluded from the provisions of the Municipal Reform Act 1835 that generally abolished old corporations. Peregrine Bingham, the Commissioner who came to investigate the Corporation in September 1833 reported; *But the defective state of its municipal institutions is said to deter respectable persons from resorting to the town, while the singular distribution of the town lands, the share assigned to the select body of the corporation, and the mode in which the select body is perpetuated, seem to have a striking tendency to unsettle industrious habits, and deprave the morals of the place.* Notwithstanding this damning indictment the Corporation survived. This was probably because Malmesbury was already benefiting from many of the services that the Act was intended to encourage [the Gasworks]. The Old Corporation remained in control of the borough until 1886, when the Municipal Corporations Act 1883 came into force. This again caused much consternation and the Deputy High Steward, Thomas Henry Chubb (1815-1879) went to discuss the position with the Minister, Sir Charles Dilke. Once again it was agreed that Malmesbury was a unique case this time due to Athelstan's Charter. The Alderman & commoners were renamed Warden & Freemen. Although they lost their political and judicial powers, they kept their land and property. Much of the present activity of the Old Corporation concerns maintenance of these properties. In 1998 Nos. 39/41 Bristol Street were rebuilt and the cottage next to St Johns Bridge was refurbished in 2002 to banish the damp. Plaques showing the Old Corporation's seal now mark the buildings that they own.

Locally much of the dispensing of justice was administered by the Corporation. Borough Sessions presided over by the Alderman or his Deputy were held in the town from at least the beginning of the 18th Century. These courts dealt with the repair of roads and bridges, apprenticeships, the setting of poor rates and other administrative matters as well as criminal hearings. Petty Sessions for the Malmesbury hundred were heard in the town from the first half of the 19th Century. The Commission on Municipal Corporations in 1833 reported that:

The alderman and twelve capital burgesses .... form the Ruling Body of the corporation: a body, which has long ceased to answer any municipal purposes, and has exercised no function but that of returning to parliament the nominees of the patron of the borough.

From the foregoing statement, it appears that this body is self-elected, irresponsible to the inhabitants of the town, and composed chiefly of labourers without education, and of the least instructed class of retail tradesmen.

The present alderman, a pig-killer and chief magistrate of the town, is scarcely able to write his name.

The alderman-elect, Simon Pike, chief magistrate for the ensuing year, is a labouring plasterer and tiler; and can neither read or write.

Richard Neate, and Christopher Aaron, successively chief magistrates, were both of them unable to write, and had no other substance or calling than keeping a few cows.

It may be supposed that such persons, however irreproachable in their private capacity, would scarcely be competent to discharge the function of chief magistrate in a considerable town. But, whether it be owing to the singular distribution of certain town lands which prevails in Malmesbury, or to any other cause, the morals of the labouring class in that town appear to be below the standard of the neighbouring country; and among those who have served the office of chief magistrate some are not exempt from the reproach of frequent intoxication, even during their year of office.

No doubt there was some special pleading for the town because although the report of the Royal Commission in 1835 stated that; *At Malmesbury, the magistrates are often unable to write or read*, the Borough Sessions continued until 1886 when the Old Corporation lost its political power and a new panel of magistrates was formed. Prominent local citizens together with the Mayor of the Borough Council and later the Chairman of the Rural District Council became magistrates, dealing with criminal cases and licensing applications.

The Old Corporation has been associated with some famous people amongst whom are:

Thomas, Lord Wharton (1648-1715) was High Steward of the Corporation from 1690 to 1699 and obtained the Charter of 1696, returning to the same post in 1705 for another 10 years. He was a fierce leading opponent of King James and supporter of William of Orange. He wrote the catchy ballad *Lilliburlero* (music by Purcell) telling of the Irish succeeding against the English, a tune which is still used by the BBC World Service. He rebelled against his strict Presbyterian upbringing such that Lord Macaulay wrote that *to the end of his long life the wives and daughters of his nearest friends were not safe from his licentious plots. Of all liars of his time he was the most deliberate, the most inventive and the most circumstantial.*

Joseph Addison (1672-1719) became one of our MPs in 1709 on the recommendation of Thomas, Lord Wharton, whose secretary he became when the latter was appointed Lord Lieutenant of Ireland. Addison represented Malmesbury until his death. Before this he had established a reputation in literary circles having been commissioned in 1705 to write *The Campaign* to celebrate the victory at Blenheim. He contributed to the *Tatler* and in 1711 he was a co-founder of the *Spectator* for which he wrote essays that were noted for their clarity, wit and elegance. However there is no record that he had any personal associations with the town.

Charles James Fox (1749-1806) was the second son of the Right Honourable Henry Fox, created Baron Holland of Foxley in 1763, who owned Norton Manor. Henry was High Steward from 1750 until 1762 as well as being a Privy Councillor and Secretary of State for War. At this time the town's MPs came from great Whig families who were rarely directly associated with Malmesbury. Charles was High Steward from 1769 to 1775 and was one of the town's MPs elected in 1774, having previously represented another rotten borough, Midhurst, at the tender age of 19. He resigned his Malmesbury seat after only a year in protest at the Government's treatment of the American colonies. He later became a supporter of Parliamentary Reform particularly advocating disenfranchising rotten and pocket boroughs to redistribute those seats to the growing industrial towns.

Joseph Pitt (1759-1842). When Thomas Estcourt gave up as High Steward in 1812 the Earl of Peterborough again tried to gain election but was defeated by Joseph Pitt, 10 votes to 2. Joseph Pitt was a self-made man, born to yeoman parents in Little Witcombe (near Birdlip). His early career was described by Lord Campbell, later Lord Chief Justice, in 1812 thus; *Pitt used to hold gentlemen*'s *horses for a penny when, appearing a sharp lad, an attorney at Cirencester took a fancy to him and bred him to his own business. He soon scraped together a little money by his practice in the law and by degrees entered into speculation ... Everything has thriven with him. He has now a clear landed estate of £20,000 a year ...* He became a solicitor in 1780 and by 1800 he was rich enough to purchase a large amount of land in Cheltenham where he planned to build a new town to rival that spa town. Between 1825 and 1830 he completed the first part of this project, the Pittville Pump Room. Unfortunately this failed to prosper and after his death was sold to the local council. He also bought much property including Eastcourt House as well as many of the houses in Cricklade, becoming one of that pocket borough's MPs due to his property ownership. As High Steward of our Corporation he became the 'borough monger' and thus controlled the representation not only of Malmesbury and Cricklade but also Wootton Bassett. In Wootton Bassett he had to pay between 20 and 45 guineas each to purchase the votes of the 309 electors. Pitt steered through the reorganisation of the Corporation in 1820. He was a rich man and the Alderman and Burgesses were known as Pitt Pensioners because of the annuities he paid them. He was associated with the bank of Pitt & Co that had branches in Bristol, Cheltenham and Cirencester. Unfortunately he backed a number of unsuccessful businesses and had to sell Eastcourt House along with other properties. He died in 1842 aged 83 and is buried in All Saints Church, Crudwell where there is a memorial in the north east corner of the church. On his death he owed £150,000 and his estate was administered by the Court of Chancery. In 1826 he was succeeded as High Steward by his son also named Joseph who held the post until 1842. Another son, Charles, was the vicar of the Abbey from 1829 until 1874. Charles and his wife Theresa Elizabeth (1812-1888) had 8 children, one of whom Charles Wightwick Pitt (1843-1914) played a prominent role as a surgeon in Malmesbury.

Through the metal gateway towards the river is the site of the:

Gasworks

The only parts of the Gasworks remaining are the coal store, used as a garage, immediately on the right, and the meter room in front of you. The gasworks was one of the benefits that resulted from *An Act for Paving the Footways, and for Cleansing, Lighting, and Regulating the Streets, and other public passages and places within the Borough of Malmesbury, in the County of Wilts; and the Avenues leading into the same; and for Removing and Preventing Nuisances, Annoyances, and Obstructions therein*, 1798 sponsored by the Corporation. Improvement Commissioners collected 'Poor Law Rates' of 6d. in the pound from all householders in the Borough and collected Sunday tolls at all the turnpike gates levied on animals coming to and from the town except for those

A professional study of the gas-lit Market Cross by William Barrett of Cirencester taken around 1950. You can just see the bracket of the street light on the corner of 1 High Street on the left which was not lit for the photograph. There is another picture showing it on page 11. The Abbey lighting was electric.

One of the 4 sets of gas lamps that provided the illumination for the Market Cross. This one is outside the Co-op at 2 High Street, the others were outside Norman Lewis Jeweller at No. 1 High Street, Fred Day Butcher at 1 Gloucester Street and Clark & Smith Solicitor 1 Oxford Street. Cecil Exton who was responsible for keeping the town's 102 street lights lit in the early 1950s is on the right.

taking people to church. They started a drainage network, arranged for cleansing of the streets and laid pavements. One interesting Clause in the Act reads; *That all Persons inhabiting within the said Borough, shall, from and after the passing of this Act, sweep, scrape, and clean the Footways before their respective Houses, Buildings, Walls, and Premises..... on every Saturday ...* Perhaps this needs to be re-enacted!

In 1836 the Commissioners encouraged the formation of the Malmesbury Gas & Coke Company and began to erect gas streetlights, often outside Commissioner's premises! The public supply of gas had only begun 25 years before in London with the first provincial scheme beginning in 1816 so once again the town were pioneers of new technology. Latterly there were three coke ovens to produce the gas which was stored in two gasometers. Pressure was maintained by placing lead weights on top of a small tank in the meter room. The Company was taken over by the South Western Gas Corporation whose offer was recommended for acceptance by the Committee of Management on 1st November 1934. In the mid 1950s the coke ovens closed and town gas was piped from Gloucester. The introduction of natural gas that began in the late 1960s led to the gasometers being demolished.

Almshouses

These attractive buildings are on the corner of St Johns Street and facing the High Street is a 12th Century archway originally part of the Hospital of St. John the Baptist which was incorporated when the structure was rebuilt in 1694. There was a chapel here in Saxon times and by the 13th Century the hospital was established. After the Knights Hospitalers were suppressed by King Henry VIII in 1540 the Corporation bought the site for £26 13s. 4d. The almshouses existed in 1622 and soon after then the Corporation was

The Almshouses before they fell into disrepair in the middle of the 20th Century. The School Arch is on the left.

organising maintenance. The building was derelict from the early 1950s until restored in 1968. Although not exactly used for its original purpose the rents for the dwellings, owned by the Old Corporation, are less than the market value. The plaque over the arch reads:

Memerand that whereas King Athelstan
did give unto the free school within this
Burrough of Malmesbury Ten Pounds and to
the poor people my Almshouse at St John's.
Ten Pounds to be paid yearly by ye Aldermen
and Burgesses of ye same Burrough for Ever.
That now Michael Weekes Esquire, late of
this said burr, and now citizen of London,
hath augmented & added to ye afore sd gift.
viz, to ye sd Free School, Ten Pounds, and to ye
sd Almshouse, Ten Pounds only, to be paid
yearly at St John's, afore sd, within this sd
burr, and by his Trustees for ever, and hath
also given to ye Minister of this Towne
for ye time being 20s only, by ye year for life
to preach a sermon yearly on ye 19th day
of July, and to his sd Trustees 20s by the
year beginning on ye 25th day of March,
Anno Dom 1694.

St John's Bridge to Market Cross

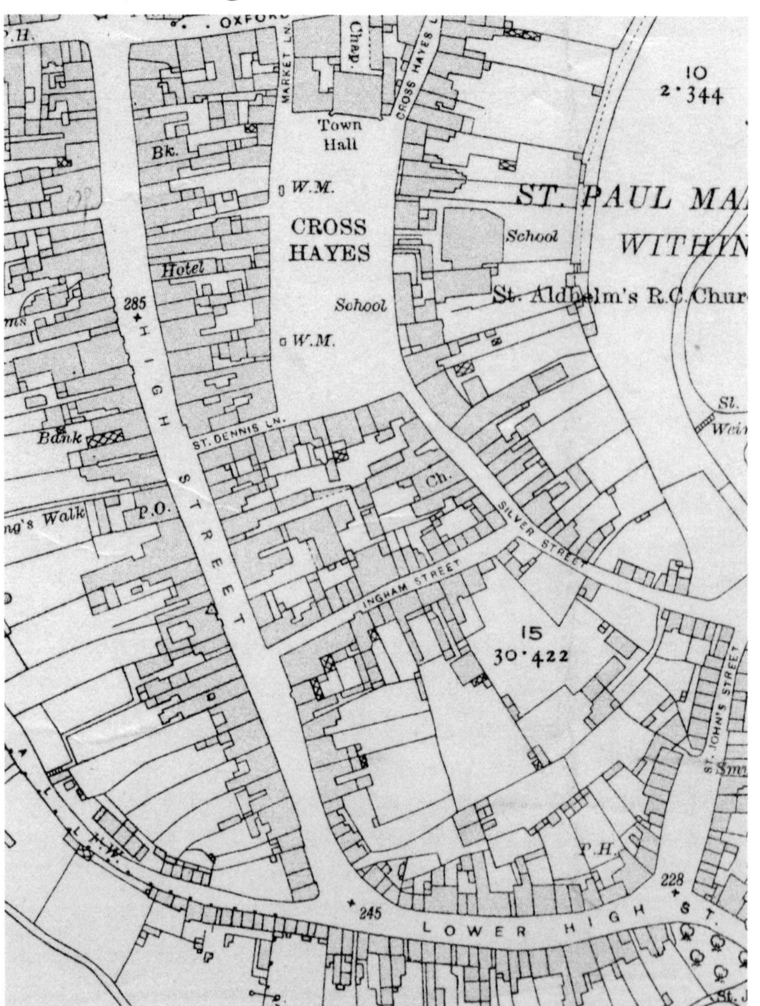

Most changes in this area have taken place at the rear of High Street premises. For example extensions have been added to Lloyds Bank (marked Bank opposite St. Dennis Lane) and the Post Office. In the 1930s new garage premises were built on the Cross Hayes side of No. 30 (just to the right of 285 on the map - now Hyams). Also a house has been built behind the Post Office along King's Walk. Before the Second World War St. Dennis Lane was doubled in width by demolishing premises on its northern side. Just south of this junction Nos. 36 and 38 have been combined, presently occupied by the Sports & Leisure shop.

On this part of the tour we will ignore the bridge but if you wish you could start the St John's Bridge to Burton Hill part of the second walk here. For now we turn right and follow the High Street immediately seeing:

Rose & Crown Inn, 102 High Street

This is an 18th Century building which had this name first as a private house and then as a pub since at least 1830. Look out to the left of the doorway for the etched window with the Stroud Brewery's name. The number of public houses and hotels described in this book with their brief histories reveals how important these institutions are in England. Dr. Hodge estimated that there were 32 hostelries open about a hundred years ago and this begs the question why there were so many in so small a town. Being on an important route from the 16th to 19th Centuries, coaching inns acted as hotels, refreshment rooms

The windows of the Rose and Crown have been enlarged and the road surfaced but nothing else seems to have changed.

and places to change horses. Taverns were the places to do business, particularly on market days. Despite innumerable wells in the town, most working people would drink ale with their meals until relatively recently, as ale was safer than untreated water. Barm (literally froth) houses would brew their own beer and might allow you to drink it in the front room. Innkeepers also offered other services, maybe a pony and trap for hire, an ostler to look after your horse or a bus to take you to a nearby town.

Since 1869 the licensing of premises to sell alcohol has been the responsibility of magistrates and that date was the start of an era of restrictions which have only recently been eased. At the end of the 19th Century the temperance movement was developing and remained a strong force until the 1930s. The Government became concerned about drunkenness which led to the Habitual Drunkards Act of 1879 and a series of Inebriates Acts in 1888, 1898 and 1899. The 1902 Licensing Act established compensation funds for licensees who were refused renewal of their licence due to the desire to encourage temperance and these were funded by a levy on all licensed premises. Licence duties were raised considerably in 1909 and again at the start of World War I. In 1915 the Government introduced very restricted licensing hours, including a gap during the afternoon when pubs had to shut which was to last for more than 80 years, to try to minimise absenteeism from munitions factories. It was also forbidden to buy drinks for anyone else. Two years later reductions were ordered in the gravity of beers to reduce their alcoholic strength. Beer consumption had halved by the war's end. The Licensing Act 1921 continued the restricted hours imposed during wartime. Only in 1988 was there a substantial relaxation of licensing hours with opening allowed between 11am and 11pm each weekday, with noon until 3pm and 7pm to 10.30pm on Sundays. You will note that not much is said about many of the pubs that are still open. To find out more you will have to visit each and buy the publican a drink!

133 High Street

An early 17th Century building with the front rebuilt in 1835. From the middle of the 19th Century it became the American Volunteer Inn, later shortened to just the Volunteer but this closed in 1922. It was then bought by Matthew Thompson, a temperance follower, who auctioned it in 1929 with a covenant that it was not to be used for the sale of beer or spirits. There are a number of pubs that closed in 1922 and it must be that when Stroud Brewery took over Duck's they rationalised their network.

92 High Street

This building has been altered many times over the years. It probably started off in the 14th Century as a house side on to the road. During the 17th Century it was a coaching inn called the Unicorn, note the large upper windows with eyebrow mouldings of that period. There was a large courtyard behind. That was the site of Malmesbury's first purpose built cinema run by a traction engine. In about 1938 a new automated telephone exchange was built in the yard and although fully equipped it was not used until after the war. The Post Office engineers were busy with the Defence Telephone Network with so

62 High Street in 1964, 2 years before it reopened as the Old Greyhound. The Cyclists Touring Club emblem can be seen.

many new military bases that very little time could be devoted to the civilian system. Around this time there were about 150 subscribers, mostly businesses with few in private houses. Shortly after 1980 a new generation electronic exchange was built at Burton Hill and the old site closed. Since 1992 Andrew P. and J.D. Poynton have run the Town Forge on the old exchange site. In February 1999 Andrew Poynton became one of only 44 Fellows of the Worshipful Company of Farriers. The house was used by Ekco workers [Cowbridge House] during the Second World War when it was split into 3 separate dwellings. Now restored to one it is privately occupied and is Grade II* listed.

Smoking Dog, 62 High Street
Built c1762 as a house, this then became the Greyhound Inn from at least 1803 to later than 1875. Henry Long was the owner in the 1870s and ran an omnibus from here to Chippenham until competition from the railway forced him out of that business (he was previously publican of the Green Dragon, Market Cross which had been the pick up point). At the end of the 19th Century it became a cafe and temperance hotel originally run by Charles Wynn. It later became the Avon Cafe until 1986. Whilst a temperance hotel it was a Cyclists Touring Club (the name adopted in 1883 by the Bicycle Touring Club of Great Britain which was formed in Harrogate on 5th August 1878) hostel where a room could be had for 2/6d. Their emblem remains on the outside wall. It reopened as the Old Greyhound Inn in 1986 and was renamed the Smoking Dog in 1989.

Forrester and Forrester, 59 High Street
The firm of Forrester and Forrester has been practising in the town since at least the early 1790s under a variety of names. Henry Gale, the first of the antecedents, sold his practice to William Stephen Jones (1817-1898) in 1849. Jones had opened an office in Cross Hayes in 1846 and five years later moved to 59 High Street which is still occupied by the practice. William Forrester (b1833) was admitted as a solicitor in 1855 and entered into a partnership with Jones in 1858. Charles Forbes Moir (1861-1928) came to the town in 1886, joined as a partner and the practice became Forrester, Moir & Company. William Forrester married twice and had six sons, two of whom were solicitors but only the eldest, Arthur Livesey (1870-1936) stayed with the firm. He originally started a career in engineering but took to the law in 1897. He joined the firm in 1902, when he was admitted as a solicitor but his father died in the same year during his third term as Mayor. Reginald Arthur Collingwood Forrester (b1907), Arthur's son, became a solicitor in 1932. Moir had a son who was a solicitor but he chose to work in London. The firm changed its name to Forrester and Forrester.

In 1935 Reginald opened an office in Chippenham. At the same time Chubb & Sons [Priory] who had practised in Malmesbury for well over 100 years were taken over. Unfortunately Arthur was killed the following year when he was living at the Old Bell. He was found one morning lying in the yard apparently having fallen from the window of his first floor bedroom. Reginald remained the sole partner for the next 10 years. After the war Derek Williamson joined him to run the Malmesbury branch. In 1959 he died whilst at his desk eating sandwiches. James Toogood was persuaded to join the firm from Robbins Olivey who acted as London agents for Forrester & Forrester. For many years articled clerks spent six months in London with Robbins Olivey to widen their experience. In 1961 Toogood and John Burridge became partners. The Chippenham office has expanded through acquisition, notably Keary, Stokes & White in 1962, a large Chippenham practice started in the 18th Century which had an office at Corsham. Another office was opened in Tetbury in 1974, but both it and the one at Corsham were closed in 1990. Reginald retired in 1977 and died in 1999 but his daughter did not wish to pursue the same career to maintain the family connection.

Bear Inn, 53 High Street

One of the town's coaching inns, it became the Bear in the late 1830s but closed in 1963. A mid 18th Century building, the frontage is now occupied by the Strakers Estate Agents and the Malmesbury Standard with a number of other businesses around the courtyard behind.

The Wilts & Gloucestershire Standard was founded to further Conservative interests in North Wiltshire and the adjoining part of Gloucestershire. The first edition was published on Saturday, 28 January 1837 and printed at the Standard Printing Works, Oxford Street, Malmesbury. The paper comprised four pages with six columns to the page and cost 5d. (2p), a large sum in those days, but 4d. represented tax, part of the so-called Taxes on Knowledge. In July 1840 the paper moved to Cirencester. The Company was taken over in 1852 and lost its political allegiance. A change of owner in 1869 led to it again being an outspoken supporter of the Tories. 1959 saw ownership pass to the Bailey Newspaper Group. They began a Malmesbury and Tetbury edition of the paper in 1984 with an office at 35, Cross Hayes. In 1995 Malmesbury once again had its own edition of the paper, an office at 53, High Street with a resident local reporter. The Bailey family sold the company to Southern Newspapers in 1998 and six months after their take-over they announced that the printing plant at Dursley was to shut with production transferred to Weymouth.

Hamptons International Estate Agents, 52 High Street

During the 18th Century the White Horse Inn was on this site It was turned into a grocery shop by Thomas Rogers in 1827. He carried on until he died in 1865. Then brothers Alfred (1841-1912) and Albert Adye (1854-1932) took it over. They were the sons of William (1792-1867) who was born in Dover but married a Malmesbury woman and set up in the High Street as a Brazier. His other two sons Sidney (1838-1910) and William (1843-1929) were also Braziers, Coppersmiths and Tin-platers at 100 and 75 High Street respectively. It would be interesting to know why part of the family moved into such a different business!

In 1877 Alfred joined his neighbour, Thomas Lot Hinwood (1838-1926) [37/39 High Street] in forming Adye & Hinwood Ltd. to build the bacon factory [Willow View

Adyes' original premises pictured around 1880.

The rebuilt premises around 1905.

Close]. To raise capital Alfred sold his share to Albert for £929 2s. 7d. which was payable in instalments with the final payment made on 29th April 1882. Alfred remained the owner of the premises and rent of 16s. per week was paid. Around the turn of the century the Grocer's name was changed to Adye and Son. Between April 1900 and July 1901 the shop was substantially rebuilt with three storeys instead of two. Henry Wilkins of the High Street was the contractor and the total bill came to £1,204 16s. 6d. One of the boasts of the business was *No foreign Bacon or Cheese ever enters these premises.*

After the Great War Albert's son Sydney assisted his father. In 1930 they took over the business of Henry

Farrant (but not his premises which they sold) from 26 High Street. More staff had to be taken on to deal with the extra customers and the experiences of Betty Richards when 15 years old can be read on the Jackdaw web-site. Albert died in 1932. After the last war it was the turn of Sydney's son David to join. Miss Ursula Luce of the Knoll was a customer who would park outside and toot her horn for service! Before the last war the Luce sisters distributed vouchers worth 5s. to the poor at Christmas, which were redeemable at Adye's. David Adye retired in 1983 when the business closed. The building is now occupied by Hamptons Estate Agents.

Gable House, 46 High Street

Originally built as a house, in 2004 it is occupied by the town's Doctors' surgery. The building is dated 1671 with 18th Century and c1890 rear extensions and the interior was rebuilt behind the facade in the mid 1980s. After the WDU [43/43a High Street] vacated these premises in the late 1940s E.A. Hider, a builder, took them over. This firm became P.J. Hider Ltd. around 1970 when they moved into No. 44 next door. Towards the end of the 1980s the building was put up for sale and eventually the doctors moved in.

At the beginning of the 20th Century the General Practitioners in town were R. Kinneir of Tower House, P.H. Nutting LRCP of Mundens, Abbey Row and C.W. Pitt MRCS [son of Revd. Charles - Old Court House] at 10 Gloucester Street. These three practices split the area around the town between them. Tower House covered the north and east, Mundens the south and Gloucester Street the west. The much loved Dr. Bernulf Hodge joined Dr. Pitt in Gloucester Street at the beginning of the 1930s and continued to practise for another 40 years. On joining as a junior doctor, Dr. Hodge was apparently obliged to take his meals in the house but only after Dr. Pitt and his family had eaten! The surgery at Mundens combined with that of Gloucester Street and eventually moved to Prospect House, Olivers Lane. The practice in Tower House continued until Dr. Michael Pym moved it into Laystalls, Cross Hayes (now occupied by the Investment Centre) in 1980. When Prospect House ran out of space new premises were needed. Unfortunately the asking price for Gable House was too high. The project was only made possible by the practices combining and premises at the rear being rented out as the Family Health Centre. The new practice with eight doctors, four nurses and up to 20 administrative staff opened in 1988. The Family Health Centre, run by the Kennet & North Wiltshire Primary Care Trust, has District Nurses, Health Visitors, a School Nurse and many other specialists either based there or regular visitors. It is planned to move all of these health care facilities to Burton Hill.

Before leaving the surgery here are a few anecdotes concerning the medical profession. Compared with today when home visits are rare, local doctors used to have 'Round Days' when they would drive around different areas on different days. If you wanted the doctor to call, a red flag or red cloth left in the hedgerow alerted him to your need. Woe betide a doctor who ignored this summons. Even during the heavy snow of January 1963 Dr. Hugh Penman used skis to visit patients in Minety. In the days before the 'Patients

Charter', the doctor was supposed to be omniscient. About a hundred years ago a friend of Harry Jones, landlord of the Kings Arms, sent for his Doctor. On arrival Dr. Pitt said "I believe he is dead". The friend immediately retorted "I beant dead", whereupon his wife said "Be quiet Oliver, the Doctor knows better than you". Later a prominent solicitor in the town telephoned Dr. Willie Winch to say that a man had died in his office. The reply was: "Did you present him with the bill?"!

43/43a & 44 High Street

Originally 43/43a was a pair of houses built in the late 18th Century but is now one house and a shop. They are constructed of limestone rubble with a brick right-hand party wall stack and stone slate roof. John Edward Ponting (1834-1906) moved to Malmesbury from Bristol before 1875. He was originally a brickmaker and timber merchant but his business expanded to incorporate builders, carpenters, painters, blacksmith, tinsmith and shops that sold furniture, carpets, china, glass and ironmongery. In the 1890s he lived at No. 43 behind which he built a large furniture warehouse. Although there was access from Kings Wall up the slope still at the west end of Kings Walk (how could you manoeuvre a horse and cart there?) one can imagine suites of furniture being moved from the street through No. 43 into the warehouse and up the stairs – the men of yesteryear must have been strong! He later bought No. 44 on the other side of the street and rebuilt that in 1901. He also intended to redevelop No. 46 which was known as the Cannon Works because of two cannons in the entrance. For some reason he did not but established a large working area at the back extending into Ingram Street for trades of nearly every description as well as two electricity generators which were not very reliable.

J.E. Pontings premises at 44 High Street is in the centre. Hanks' Stationers occupied No. 42 until around 1930.

JOHN EDWARD PONTING,

MALMESBURY,

FURNISHING IRONMONGER & CUTLER,

Oil, Colour, Lead & Glass Merchant,

AGRICULTURAL IMPLEMENT AGENT.

MAKER OF DAIRY UTENSILS, AND TIN, BRASS, COPPER, ZINC, AND IRON GOODS.

BUILDERS' IRONMONGER.

Sanitary Pipes	Blue Paving and Stable Bricks
Bends	Terra Cotta Chimney Tops
Junctions	Roofing Slates and Cress
Syphons	White Lime
Closet Pans and Traps	Cement
Sink Stones and Troughs	Plaster of Paris
Pennant Stones	Fire Clay and Plasterers' Hair
Hearth Stones and Freestone	Oak and Deal Laths
Fire Bricks	Slate and Pantile Laths
Burrs and Squares	Roofing Felt, &c., &c.

MAKER OF

Builders' Bricks Cress Flower Pots and Saucers
Pipes Seed Pans Rhubarb and Seakale Pots
Tiles Chimney Pots Strawberry & Garden Border Tiles, &c., &c.

An advert from the 1882 Kellys Directory demonstrating the wide variety of goods available from Pontings. This range expanded over time.

Four sons and many other relatives were employed in the businesses which owned other High Street premises and several cottages in Ingram Street. Unfortunately the whole enterprise was put into voluntary liquidation in 1940. All of the premises were taken over by the Western Development Unit (WDU) of E.K. Cole Ltd [Cowbridge House]. Because of the secrecy surrounding their development work on radar many rumours persisted about the work that they were doing. I was told over 50 years later that ammunition was being produced in the centre of town! In fact it was more mundane. The old furniture warehouse was used to test air interception radar sets – there was an aerial in a small greenhouse type structure on its roof that pointed at a reflector at Lea. WDU moved to the Swindon Road factory in 1946. Since then Nos. 43 and 43a have been occupied by many different types of shop. No. 44 was used as Wiltshire County Council's library from 1953 to 1967 after which it too was used for a variety of shops until Stitchcraft moved in during 1985.

Post Office, 41 High Street

During the 18th Century there was a pub here called the White Swan. A timetable of 1773 showed that a coach left here for Holborn Bridge, London every Wednesday. The pub closed around 1800 and the building was split into tenements either side of Berry's Entry, so called after the proprietor of the property. J.E. Ponting bought the tenements before the end of the 19th Century and built the Post Office there completing it in 1902. The Ponting family leased this building to the Post Office until they sold the freehold many years later. There was a full service here until 1990. Post Office Counters then moved their operation into the Circle-K (now Co-operative) Supermarket at 8 High Street. In August 1999 the Post Office announced that it was hoping to relocate the Sorting Office to the outskirts of the town but at the time of writing is still seeking a site. The first reference I have found to a Post Office in Malmesbury is in the Pigot's Directory of 1830 when Henry Garlick Hanks (1789-1879) of the High Street was Postmaster. He ran a watch and clockmakers at 33 High Street. At the end of the 19th Century the premises were provided by Francis Herbert Summers, photographer and stationer next door at 31 High Street.

In 1900 the postmistress was Miss Ruth Bartlett (1859-1902) at Summers' shop. Mails arrived three times a day and there were three deliveries each weekday with one on Sundays. There were wall letterboxes at the Triangle, the Railway Station, and Burton Hill. Each had five collections a day with one on Sundays except for Burton Hill, which had no Sunday collection. Money orders were granted and paid between 8am and 8pm each weekday.

Telephone

The telegraph system preceded the development of telephones. Before Malmesbury had its own telegraph office telegrams for residents of the town were sent to the railway station at Minety and then conveyed by a Post Office employee on horseback. This cost 1s. per mile, or 7s. for the whole journey. I have been unable to establish exactly when our own Post Office was connected to the system but it seems to have been about 1870, probably when the railway arrived. The General Post Office took over the Telegraph Companies in 1870 (an early example of nationalisation) and began their own telephone system in 1881. Their main competitor, the National Telephone Company, was taken over in 1912. The GPO had a small telephone network in Malmesbury by 1906 with 28 subscribers – the Earl of Suffolk had three lines! Certainly later there was a manual exchange on the first floor of the Post Office. This exchange covered a wide area from Shipton Moyne in the west to the Somerfords in the east. A new exchange in Lower High Street opened in the late 1940s.

Boots & Geddes Carpets, 37/39 High Street

In the middle of the 19th Century Thomas Lot Hinwood came to Malmesbury from Ramsbury to open a Linen Draper's in the High Street. Later Thomas concentrated on the Bacon curing business and moved to Ferndale Terrace, 85 Gloucester Road. One of his sons Frederick Louis (1865-1901) took over the gentleman's outfitters at 39 High Street above which his family lived. The name of the business was now Hinwood and Son. Frederick died shortly after the turn of the century of tuberculosis. His widow, Martha, carried the business on until Harry Hinwood joined and as it expanded number took over 37 High Street. By 1923 their adverts proclaimed that they were outfitters and tailors who specialised in sports wear. In 1949 Jim Thornbury joined the business. The shop was a favourite with children as it had a pneumatic tube to shoot the takings to the cash office.

Mr. Thornbury bought the business in 1969 by which time No. 39 had been sold. He continued until December 1994 when the premises were sold. No. 39 became a furniture shop, then a shop selling antiques, a restaurant and coffee shop until in 1993 it was taken over by Boots the Chemist who had occupied No. 19 since 1939. Geddes Carpets have traded from No. 37 since 1995, having previously been at No. 47.

During 2003 the upper stories of No. 39 were renovated. This revealed that the building dates back to c1500. Originally two timber framed houses each with a single central

This seems to be the funeral procession of Colonel Charles Miles in 1918. Note the narrowness of St. Dennis Lane.

window on each of the upper two floors of the gables which were jettied into the street. It is believed that these façades were highly decorated. In the 18th Century the frames were cut back to align with the ground floor to create a single typically Georgian frontage.

Malmesbury Rendezvous, 34 High Street
There was a pub here called the Crown & Ball with origins at the beginning of the 19th Century but in 1842 it was just called the Crown. For much of the first half of the 20th Century it was in use as a butchers shop, owned for part of this time by Tom Rich who moved here from No. 27 during the First World War. Just prior to World War II a good part of the building was demolished for the widening of St Dennis Lane. What remains has been occupied by the somewhat incongruously named Malmesbury Rendezvous Chinese take-away (which used to be called more appropriately the Oriental Chef) since 1994.

Lloyds TSB Bank, 35 High Street
The first bank in Malmesbury was opened at the beginning of the 19th Century somewhere in St Dennis Lane. The proprietors were Messrs Hanks, the Deputy High Steward, Ody, Smith, both brewers, Richard Robins (1762-1836), a solicitor and Young, the owner of a cloth mill at Cowbridge. They issued banknotes payable at their premises in Malmesbury or at Pastons, Cockerell, Trail & Company, Pall Mall, London. They recruited Thomas Luce (1790-1875) as Manager in 1813 who moved to the town from Dorset. Thomas later became a partner when the name changed to Robins, Luce and

Young. Not long after that he became the sole owner. However in 1836 he sold the business to the Wilts and Dorset Banking Company. That bank was founded in Salisbury the previous year and was seeking to expand quickly. Thomas was retained as branch manager living at the bank and his son, Charles took over from him in 1863. In 1914 the Wilts and Dorset was taken over by Lloyds Bank and after the First World War when that Company took over Capital and Counties they had two branches in the High Street. 35 High Street was rebuilt in 1924 and the branch at No. 10 closed.

Hyams Autos Ltd., 26 High Street

Henry Farrant (1864-1933) had a grocer's shop here from at least 1889 to 1930. Around 1900 the shop included an off-licence that advertised the products of W.A. Gilbey, from Crudwell. Farrant was known as 'Split Fig' as he would do that to make the correct weight. His turnover in 1928 was £7,373 and £6,857 the following year when his wage bill came to £443 12s. 11d. He retired at the age of 66 in 1930 and sold the business to Adye & Son. They did not want the premises and sold them to E.S.T. Cole Ltd. who had been at No. 25 opposite since 1920.

Edwin Stuart Travis (Stuart) Cole (1894-1984) was a RAF pilot in World War I. On his return from the war he started a motor dealership at 52 Gloucester Street, which still retains a shop front although it has been a private house for years, before moving into the High Street. At No. 26 he made several innovations including the installation of the first hydraulic ramps in the South West and by using a special concrete mix for the workshop

On the left is the horse bus with a sign reading Henry Jones that met every train at the Railway Station. Sun screens to protect stock obscure Farrant's to the right. In the background neither Knees nor Midland Bank have yet been built.

floor to stop it absorbing oil. His son Richard Stuart Travis (Dick) Cole (1918-1988) continued running this prestigious dealership until the early 1970s when it amalgamated with Tony Lloyd Jones' Athelstan Garage. Car sales continued here for a couple of years but the greater space available on the corner of Gloucester Road and Park Road caused the business to concentrate there and sell this site.

The buyers were Mrs. Joan Hyams and her son Paul. They had no previous experience of the motor trade, Paul having been an apprentice electrician who became a burglar alarm engineer! Initially they traded second hand cars but slowly recruited a number of mechanics and became Renault dealers in 1982. In 1998 they changed to being dealers for Ford and Marcos.

Kings Arms Hotel, 29 High Street

A late 16th or early 17th Century inn re-named for the restoration of Charles II. The timber bay windows are 18th Century additions. Its yard used to extend to Olivers Lane, where the flying monk Eilmer is said to have landed in 1010. This was a popular farmers' pub where much money changed hands on market days. The yard was the equivalent of a modern car park - horses & coaches were left here whilst their owners went about their business. Even up until the 1920s an ostler was based here. It is said that Sir Ronald Bouchier, a Royalist Cavalier who carried messages between Bristol and Oxford was murdered whilst staying here overnight. His ghost apparently haunts the room above the archway. A rather tall ghost story was recounted in the Daily Mirror of 17th June 1935 which is reproduced in Stan Hudson's book, *A Hilltop Town*, or visit the pub and look at

Mr. & Mrs. Jones, she became licensee after his death. Tom Rich's early premises are on the right.

the press cuttings on the first floor landing.

On 30th May 1831 this was the venue for a dinner for supporters of the Reform Bill. There were 140 guests including the borough-monger, Joseph Pitt. The speakers did not pull their punches – the Chairman, George Powlet Scrope must have made Mr. Pitt uncomfortable with; *The Boroughmonger, Gentlemen, is an animal of unclean habits and vicious propensities. Like the swine, he is fond of wallowing in the mire, and corruption is his natural element. He has the ravenous appetite of the wolf; but he has also many qualities of the ass, so that naturalists are undecided to which of these genera to refer him, partaking as he does of all three.* R. Gordon MP for Cricklade included these words; *Even in the County of Wilts, where there are so many sinks of impurity and corruption, the Borough of Malmesbury stands pre-eminent*, and John Lewis; *This Borough, the rottenest of all other rotten boroughs, must ..... be cleansed of the impurity with which it has been so long deluded.*

Harry Jones (1853-1911) took over as the landlord in 1880 after the death of his father Thomas who was the previous licensee. Harry became very famous and was often pictured wearing a tall hat. He was Mayor in 1885 and started the custom of having an annual Civic Church Service as well as being the first to wear robes of office. Letters addressed to 'Harry Jones, England' or merely with a drawing of his trademark top hat were correctly delivered. Edward VII called in whenever he was in the area. The path by the Post Office between the High Street and Kings Wall was to be called King Edward

The upper High Street in the 1920s with only one parked car! The London Joint City & Midland Bank premises on the left was built in 1923 on the site of Frederick Compton (1838-1920) Draper's shop. The name of the bank changed to Midland in 1932 and HSBC 60 years later. The George Hotel is on the right.

the Seventh's Walk, but this was too much of a mouthful and was shortened to King's Walk.

The George Veterinary Hospital, 20 High Street

The George Hotel was a coaching inn with origins in the 16th Century and the present building dates from 1788. Richard Jefferies in 1867 wrote; *The George Commercial Hotel, where good accommodation can be obtained for man and horse at moderate charges, and where the antiquary may congratulate himself upon residing in a house that has been established nearly two centuries*. The main doorway was originally an open archway allowing coaches through the building and wheel ruts can still be seen. After the hotel closed Messrs. Oura, Griffin and Bown moved their veterinary practice here in 1978. The practice started in the 1930s when Major Tindle began a horse practice working from Quarry House, Corston. Mr. L. 'Nipper' Constance who had been invalided out of the Royal Army Veterinary Corps joined him in 1942. Treating cattle and (unusually for the time) small animals, Nipper operated from Rodbourne, moving to Lea and finally in 1949 to Burnham House, Malmesbury. Just after the end of the war Peter Oura joined. When Mr. Constance left the partnership in 1964 to run a horse practice in Didmarton, Peter became the sole partner assisted by Roger Griffin who had joined a couple of years before. Burnham House was sold and the practice continued from 97 Gloucester Road where Mr. Griffin became a partner. Peter Bown became an assistant in 1968 and later the junior partner. The practice was renamed the George Veterinary Hospital after the move and in the 20 years since taking up residence has become a substantial business. There are branch surgeries in Wootton Bassett and Tetbury.

The premises of James May (b1840), Town Crier and Bill Poster. At this time Griffin Alley was known as May's Entry.

12-18 High Street

This was the site of the Griffin Inn. Part of the building dates back to 1390 but it is mostly of mid 16th Century origin. Aubrey reported that *Hughes of Wootton Bassett saises that the steeple of Malmesbury Abbey was as high as Paul's and that when the steeple fell, the ball of it fell as far as the Griffin*. In other words the Abbey spire was as high as St Paul's Cathedral and the golden orb at its tip ended up here when the tower collapsed in 1479. The Griffin was in use as a pub in 1540 and 1751 but it closed before 1765. The 1803 Manorial

Stan Hudson's shop with customers outside. From the right Sam Ellett who worked in Stan's office is riding the BSA 3½ motorbike and sidecar with Dick Lockstone as passenger, Douglas Lockstone on the Triumph 500 Solo with John Hislop on the pillion. Mr. E. Grabham seems to be driving the Morris Eight whilst Stan is looking at the bonnet.

survey described the building as: *a large messuage or tenement, formerly the Griffin Inn, in the Corn Market of the High Street – the front lately rebuilt with brick with extensive outbuildings and courtyard, in the occupation of Thomas Hill and son, John Hill; having a freehold house of John Player on the North, and the George Inn on the South thereof.* The pub originally straddled Griffin Alley with stables at the rear and there are a number of wooden beams and squat low doorways visible along the Alley.

Various retailers have occupied the site since including at No. 16 Stanley Walter Hudson (1897-1979). In 1929 he opened his shop originally concentrating on cycles but eventually selling motor cycles, cars, accessories and petrol. He used the slogan 'The Push 'em in and Ride 'em out Shop'. He was co-opted on to the Borough Council in 1942 and was Mayor from 1946 to 1948, serving for over 31 years. He was made a Freeman in 1974 at the same time as Dr. Hodge. Stan retired from business in 1964 although the shop was bought by Ivor Adye who traded until 1976 using Stan's name.

In the first quarter of the 20th Century Arthur Mattick, Saddler was at No. 12. He moved out after fire burnt out his premises on 28th January 1928. The middle part of the building is now occupied by Flowers Galore.

A4 Stationers, 14 High Street

This is a 16th Century building with a late 19th Century shopfront which at one time was a pub called the Black Swan and also had been part of the Griffin Inn. From the late 1880s to 1939 it was a restaurant or refreshment rooms, then a fruiterers until the 1980s. More recently it became a DIY store. A kitchen and bedding shop (Eat & Sleep) occupied it until the end of February 1999, afterwards becoming DAC Stationers, now renamed A4.

H.J. Knee Ltd., 17 High Street

These premises were built in 1902 for Jones and Son. James A. Jones (1868-1966) was Mayor in 1911, 1923-24, 1930 and 1939. At the age of 96 he was the oldest Alderman and longest serving member of any Council in Great Britain. He first had a cycle and musical instrument shop at No. 10 Oxford Street, where he was living in 1901, until he bought these premises and built the new large store. They sold bicycles, motor cars, ironmongery, furniture and musical instuments.

The store was sold around 1930 first to P.M. Rhodes, later to Mr. Richards and finally to Mr. and Mrs. Charles Hazell in 1947. It continued to trade under the name of Jones and Son. Charles Hazell was one of the sons of the Railway Hotel's licensee. He and his wife built up a very successful greengrocers business in Corsham. Shortly after the end of World War II they sold up, moved to Corston and ran this department store until retiring in 1960. H.J. Knee from Trowbridge then took over the business. Henry John Knee had opened a corner shop in Trowbridge in 1879. Originally selling ironmongery and furnishings, the business had expanded to become at one time or another a department store, removal firm, building contractor, restaurant, hairdressers, and undertakers with premises in Bradford-on-Avon and Melksham. Noel Knee, grandson of the founder, negotiated the purchase in Malmesbury and was more favourably disposed after Mrs.

Just north of Olivers Lane (so called because Eilmer is supposed to have landed here) Eastmans Butchers was demolished to make way for the larger premises of Jones & Son at the beginning of the 20th Century. All manner of goods and services were available from here - H.J. Knee continue in the same tradition.

Hazell served him the best tea he had ever eaten! After Knees took over they knocked down some cottages at the rear and extended the shop.

10 High Street

This is a fine example of a brick building from the time of George I, 1714-27, made from 2" bricks with stone window dressings and roof parapet. In the middle of the 19th Century William Walker (1822-1900) farmed during the day but ran a bank in these premises each evening for two hours. He sold out to North Wilts Banking Company (founded in Melksham 1835) who kept him on as manager. In 1877 the company merged with the Hampshire Banking Co. and the following year changed name to Capital and Counties Bank. In 1918 the Company amalgamated with Lloyds and in 1924 this branch closed.

The offices of Malmesbury Rural District Council in 1964.

Under the Public Health Act 1872 a Rural Sanitary Authority was created which took over some responsibilities from the parishes. The Highway Act 1879 made it also the Highway Authority. The Local Government Act 1894 created district and parish councils leading to the conversion of the Rural Sanitary Authority into Malmesbury Rural District Council, which took over many more functions of the parish. The Council comprised 20 Councillors, one for each parish with a Chairman. The District encompassed a large area, from Luckington in the west, Crudwell in the north, to Dauntsey and Hullavington but excluded the town which was controlled by the Borough Council. There were three times as many people in this area than in the town. The Council originally met in the Guardians Board Room at the workhouse [Bremilham Rise]. After the bank closed they had offices at 10 High Street from the late 1920s. Many officers served both the Borough Council and the Rural District Council. For example in 1900 Montague Henry Chubb [the Priory], solicitor, was Clerk, Dr. Charles Wightwick Pitt was Medical Officer and Henry Hewer, manager of the Capital & Counties Bank, was Treasurer of both. The Mayor of the Borough Council and the Chairman of the R.D.C. both sat as magistrates.

Co-operative Store, 8 High Street

Members of the Garlick family lived at this address during the 19th and early 20th Century. They were butchers with their slaughterhouse behind the house facing on to Cross Hayes. James (1810-1891) was the occupant around 1850, followed by Henry (b1842) who was Mayor in 1893 and 1899. In the early 1960s this fine 18th Century house was demolished and a large (for the time) supermarket was built. This was part of the Fine Fare chain and the store was opened by a family of chimpanzees who featured in a series of television advertisements for PG Tips tea! John Betjeman remarked that this building was quite the most disgraceful thing on a High Street in the south of England. It was rebadged as Gateways in the mid 1980s shortly before the new store was opened in Gloucester Road [Somerfield]. From about 1987 Circle-K took over the High Street shop and their name changed to Alldays in 1994. Circle-K won the contract to run the Post Office Counters concession in 1990 when the Post Office at number 43 became just the Sorting and Delivery Office. In 2002 the Co-operative Wholesale Society took over Alldays, rebranding this store the following summer.

Hobbs & Chambers, 2 High Street

There was a pub called the Red Lion Inn here in the late 18th Century. From 1885 to 1919 Frederick Newman (1857-1934) ran his grocers business here. He rebuilt the roof of the Oxford Street part of the premises so that it was the same height as the High Street frontage. When he retired he sold to the Chippenham Co-op which closed in 1969. Since 1989 Halifax Estate Agents have been the occupiers.

It is unfortunate that the photographer was more interested in the Bullnosed Morris, but the Chippenham Co-op shop at 2 High Street can be seen in the background.

Walk 2 Abbey Row to Stainsbridge

Although Joe Moore carried out a lot of work at the Old Bell around 1908, it is evident from the map that much has been done since at the rear of the premises. The 3 cottages between the Baptist Chapel and Avon House are shown. The Triangle still has a weighing machine seemingly. Not many buildings have been put up along our route in the past 80 years, notable exceptions are Grant Barnes, Saddlers at the start of Burnham Road and Highbank next to Westport House, Gloucester Street.

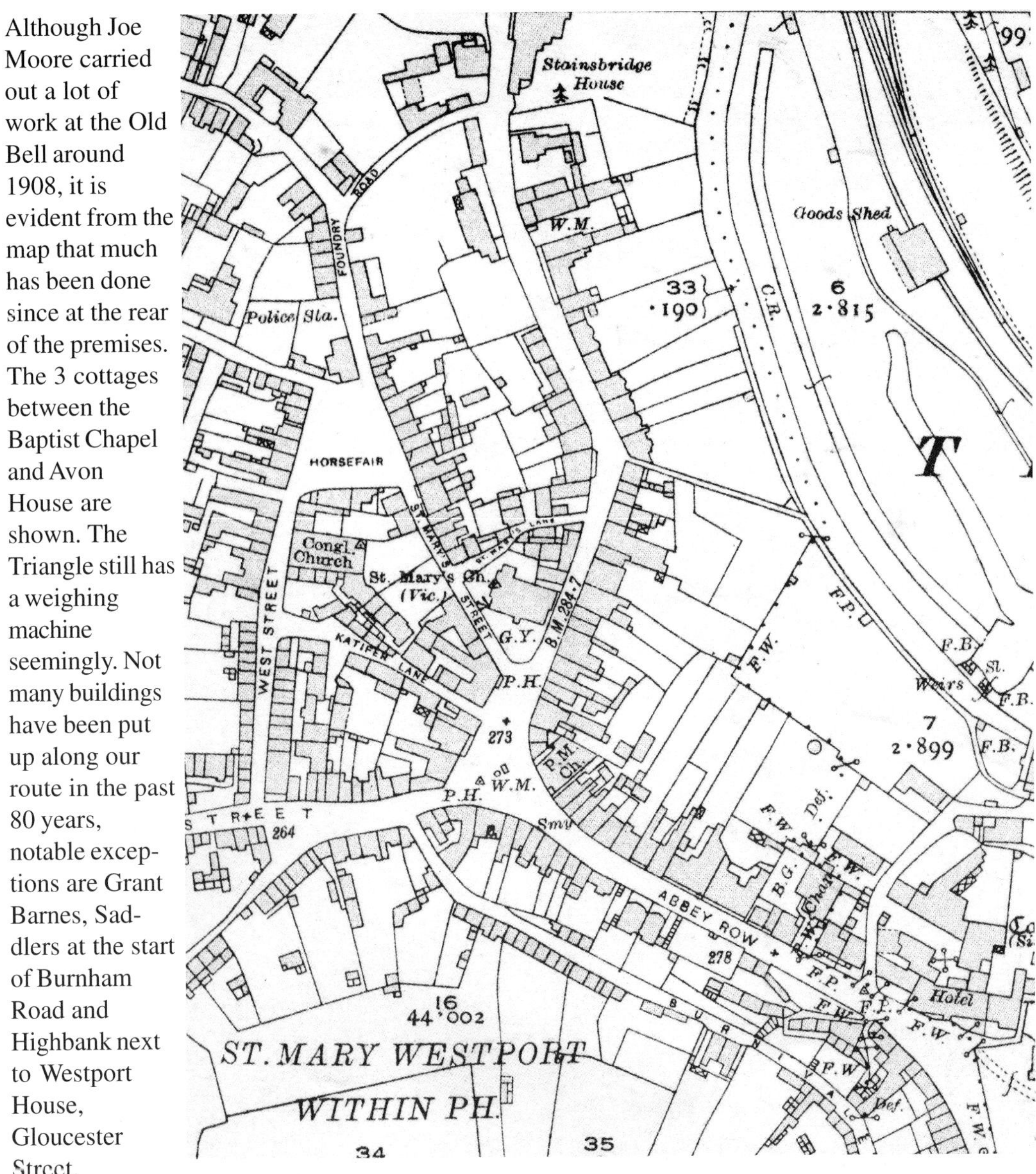

We start at the west end of the Abbey and proceed along Abbey Row. It is said that properties along this road were demolished during the Civil War so that they could not shelter snipers close to the town's walls. Later during the 18th Century it was where the boys of Westport and the town would fight, about a fortnight before the anniversary of the Gunpowder Plot. The origin of this custom is not known and there is no demand to reinstate it!

Old Bell Hotel, 13/17 Abbey Row

As the narrow ridge that carries Abbey Row is the only way that the town can be approached on the level without a water barrier this is a weak point in the natural defences and the obvious position for a fortification. Certainly it was fortified in Saxon times. Bishop Roger of Sarum upgraded the defences by building a stone castle here about 1130. It was apparently deliberately built very close to the monastery in order to upset the monks. The monks disliked the close proximity of soldiers and arranged the demolition at the first opportunity after the King gave permission in 1216. During a recent excavation when the hotel car park was extended, remains of what was probably the castle keep were found.

It is thought that Abbot Walter Loring (Abbot from 1208-1244) had a new building put up on the site of the demolished castle in around 1220 to house his important guests. Although much altered, the stone hooded fireplace in the Great Hall dates from this period. It is because the building has catered for guests continuously from then that the Old Bell claims to be England's oldest hotel. The facade dates from the 18th Century but the rear elevation is older. It has been open as a pub since at least 1703, originally known as the Castle. The name was changed to the Bell Hotel in 1798. Just after the turn of the 20th Century the owner Joseph Moore is supposed to have found a hoard of gold which enabled him to carry out extensive works. Three cottages adjoining the Bell to the west were demolished leaving only the front wall (which is still there). At the same time Castle House to the east was purchased and incorporated into the hotel. This together with a large extension to the west was completed in 1908 (see the date stone JM 1908 on the eastern chimney) and it was renamed the Old Bell Hotel. The Moore family sold the hotel in 1930 after nearly a century's ownership.

The Old Bell Hotel in 1933. What used to be Castle House is to the right of the flagpole.

Castle House was a 17th Century house occupied by two 'little Miss Luces', (Susannah Hollis 1823-1905 & Sarah Grace 1835-1887) before it was incorporated into the Bell. They kept a pony with a four-wheeled carriage and held a bible class for women every Sunday afternoon. After Susannah's death Harry Duck [32 Cross Hayes] lived here for about a year before Jo Moore bought it.

Jubilee Garden

As you pass the site of West Gate (look at the bronze plates in the pavement and on the wall of Westgate cottage) opposite the Old Bell you will see Betty Geezers Steps. These are so called because a widow named Elizabeth Gaze owned a farm near here. She walked up and down the hill nearly every day of her life and on her death gave the steps to the town. Take time to read the brass plaque with information about the West Gate on the wall of the cottage and the quotation from Sir John Betjeman in the pavement. Just below the wall is a garden owned by the Hotel which is for public use with a superb view of the river valley. This was established by Malmesbury Civic Trust (which still maintains it) to celebrate the Queen's Silver Jubilee in 1977.

Malmesbury Civic Trust was formed in 1963 when it was proposed to develop Daniel's Well – the view from this garden. Concerned residents met and the Society was formed, initially chaired by Graham Carey, Art Master at the Secondary Modern School. He also completed a comprehensive photographic study of the town the following year which is held by the National Monuments Records Centre in Swindon. Sir John Betjeman was the

A view along Abbey Row from the west early in the 20th Century. Note the terrace just beyond Avon House (left centre) with the cottage outside the Baptist Chapel next door referred to in the map commentary.

first President. The Trust negotiated with local landowners for access and then carried out much work in 1972/3 to create the River Walk. This has since been enjoyed by thousands of visitors and local walkers – for further information you can buy a colour booklet in the Town Hall. A further series of photographs was completed during the millennium year.

Abbey Row Baptists' Chapel, 23 Abbey Row

This church was formed about 1688. They quickly established the practice of baptism in the river near to Mill Lane which drew many onlookers. They originally met in a small

Only parts of the walls of the cottage in front of the Baptist Chapel now remain.

building in Abbey Row later used for stabling. The present building was put up in 1802, enlarged by adding galleries in 1814, the north end demolished and lengthened in 1816 and refurbished in 1910. It closed in the mid 1980s but was bought by the Kings Church [King's Nursery] in 1997 and once again has a vibrant congregation. There are a number of graves around the chapel with others in a graveyard on the north side of Burnham Road. The stone gate piers, railings and the gravestone of Mary and Giles Carter who died in 1823 and 1829 respectively are listed.

Avon House, 25 Abbey Row

The present Avon House, Grade II* listed, was rebuilt in 1798 with a Georgian facade on a much older smaller cottage. John Alexander (1824-1910) of Malmesbury went to America around 1850 and joined John D. Rockefeller in the fledgling oil industry. He later sold out and returned to purchase Avon House sometime around 1871. It is rather

John Alexander standing outside Avon House. The carriage house with gate on the left is now No. 25A.

ironic that having been involved in the development of a new fuel he built up a business selling coal, coke, wood, salt and artificial manure with premises in Gloucester Road as well as at Somerford and Tetbury. He is buried along with his first wife Sebella (1823-1881) and second wife Hephzibah (1843-1920) in the Abbey churchyard to the south west of the west end. His eldest son Walter (1844-1907) continued the business, living at Westport House 116 Gloucester Road opposite his coal yard at No. 97. Joseph Moore moved to Avon House with his daughters when he sold the Old Bell. One of them, Mary Moore (d1978) created 25A, the attached former carriage house, which on her death was left as a home for the elderly together with a legacy of £10,000. By 1983 it was occupied by the charity's administrator. This charity has moved and provides a parson to minister to the elderly. The main house from at least 1973 was used as a dentists by Barker, Tufft, Brown and partners, but it is now a private house.

Euclid Villas, 62 & 64 Abbey Row

These rather incongruous houses were built in 1881 by John Alexander to block his neighbour's view. He had been upset by a new building being erected in the back garden of the Mundens. Apparently the neighbour was so incensed that he sued and the case established the principle that you cannot prevent the obscuration of a view by a new building.

Mundens, 27 Abbey Row

This stone house has an inscription on a rainwater hopper on the eastern end with some initials and the date 1811. At the rear there was the purported Castle Well, now filled in. Revd. James Moffat (d1804) in his *History of Malmesbury* stated that the well was *large, of great depth and the workmanship neatly executed*. From the late 19th Century for nearly a hundred years this was one of three surgeries in the town, the others being Tower House and 10 Gloucester Street. One of the main parts of the Welfare State introduced by the Labour administration after World War II was the provision of free medical services. However it was not welcomed by all, the British Medical Association bitterly opposed it with doctors voting 9:1 against it in March 1948. A patient from Foxley wrote to Dr. Winch on the subject saying *A few years in the Civil Service and all doctors will become bureaucrats and patients just number*s and *I believe the fears are justified for it has been the avowed intention of the Socialists to have complete control over the medical services*. However the National Health Service Act 1946 created the 'nationalised' health service which was implemented with effect from 5th July 1948.

We reach the Triangle, previously called Sheepfair, a market outside the Town gates and thus not subject to the Corporation's tolls.

Looking from the end of Abbey Row you can see a gas lamp next to the weighing machine's hut in the Triangle. Just to the left of the lamp is Woodman's bakery with a delivery handcart outside and a sign over the door. At No. 37, on the right Fry's Chocolate and Pure Cocoa are advertised as well as Waverley Cigarettes 10 for 3d.

Primitive Methodist Chapel, The Triangle

Having grown out of their Bristol Street premises, this chapel was built in 1899. In 1932 they joined with the Wesleyan Methodists, who had been without a chapel since 1919 when their Oxford Street chapel had been sold, to become part of the Methodist Church. Around 1970 there was a Methodist Malmesbury Circuit comprising 13 chapels in this area. It was latterly part of the Chippenham Circuit and the congregation became so small that it closed in the summer of 2004 for conversion into a private house.

Castle House, 82 The Triangle

This was a public house that opened in 1662 as the Weavers Arms. It probably changed its name to the Castle Inn at the beginning of the 19th Century when the Old Bell Hotel no longer used that name. It was taken over by Luce's Brewery in 1890. Many Malmesbury businesses relied on agriculture which was in crisis caused by falling produce prices and poor harvests during this decade . Many other pubs were taken over by breweries at this time. Closed in 1961 it is now a private house.

First World War Memorial, The Triangle

There are a number of memorials in the town and a brief list of the most important is given here. Derek Tilney, Chairman of the Royal British Legion Branch, has done much research on this subject. The first commemorated the sixteen men who volunteered to serve in the South African War of 1899-1902 and the two who died there. There are several World War I memorials including a wooden tablet prepared for the Borough Council with 70 names on it. Both of these used to be displayed in the Tourist Information Office but are now stored in the Town Hall. The Secondary School memorial (14

The Armistice Service at the War Memorial in 1925. In the background can be seen the wall around St. Mary's Church. Note that there is no telephone kiosk (now a listed building!) on the corner of Katifer Lane.

names) was installed in the new school premises in 2003, the Abbey has a wooden shrine with two brass plaques displaying 68 names and in the Old Parish Rooms, Silver Street [Kings Nursery] the Cirencester Conservative Benefit Society memorial shows 127 of its members who served and the 13 who fell.

The main memorial is at the Triangle. The Borough Council bought the weighbridge that was previously here for £150 and latterly run by the Sealy family. The memorial was designed by B. de Bertodano [Cowbridge House] and was dedicated with much pomp on Sunday 20th March 1921. It cost £525 which was raised by public subscription. In 1988 repairs totalling £397 were completed with the cost being shared between the Town Council and British Legion. 74 men are remembered here including one civilian. He was the Rev. E.H. Davies who was the minister of the Congregational Church in St Mary's Street. In 1917 the YMCA appealed for volunteers to look after Indian troops in France. The Rev. Davies, although he had been doing sterling work as chaplain to the Red Cross Hospital and was 42 with three children, felt that as an ex missionary he was well qualified. Unfortunately within three months of arriving in France he died. The fallen of the Second World War are commemorated by a garden and gates near to the Town Bridge which are described later.

Three Cups Inn, 90 Triangle
A pub has been on this site from the 15th Century. The present building dates back to the 17th Century although it has been much altered. The right-hand rear wing was probably extended to include No. 2 St Mary's Street. In the first Elizabethan age cloth buyers and yarn sellers would stay here. The pub was reputed to have been the headquarters of General Waller in March 1643 when he was besieging the town. It also featured in a case heard in the Court of Chancery in 1702. Henry Chapman, a butcher of Westport died in 1699. He was the leaseholder of the Three Cups which was apparently worth £300 and he was 'esteemed to be a very rich man.' However he died owing money to a number of people who sued his brother in law and landlord who were alleged to have taken many of the assets of the estate. They said that Chapman was poor and that the inn was frequented by coal-wainers (carriers of coal) and travellers in summer but had little or no custom in winter. By 1930 the Stroud Brewery had renovated the pub, installed electric light and it was reported that *the old inn looks as if it is coming back into its own again*. Visit and see if it has!

49 The Triangle,
In 1596 there is mention of a grammar school in the Sheepfair opposite the Three Cups and it was probably here. The master, Robert Latimer, instructed Thomas Hobbes and later taught John Aubrey. The Oddfellows Inn on this site was supposed to have been opened in 1799 and it closed in 1922. About 10 years later it became the premises of a hairdresser and continued as such until 1980. By the early 1990s it had become a private house.

St. Marys Church with its original high stone wall around it.

St. Mary's Hall, Westport

John Aubrey [Abbey Church] described the original church as *a prettie church, where there were very good windows and a fair steeple, higher than the other* (St Paul's – the present belfry) *which much adorned the toune of Malmesbury; in it were five tuneable bells, which Sir Wm. Waller melted into Ordnance or rather sold; and the church was pilled down that the enemie might not shelter themselves against the garrison of Malmesbury. The church was dedicated to St. Mary. Here were three aisles, which took the whole area. It is reported to have been more ancient than the Abbey. In the windows, which were very good, were inscriptions which declared as much.* His description of the replacement in 1680 was *now is here rebuilt a church like a stable.*

A second aisle was added in 1840 and early in the 20th Century the seating was rear-ranged including the removal of a three-decker pulpit. The church was closed in 1946. It was used as a grammar school classroom during the late 1940s and became the Church Hall in 1977. The graveyard for St Mary's Church was in Burnham Road but was deconsecrated when Hudson Road was developed. In 2003 the 1st Malmesbury (King Athelstan) Scouts bought it.

This Scout Troop was formed in 1910 through the munificence of the de Bertodano family from Cowbridge House. Robert Baden-Powell, the defender of Mafeking during the Boer War, began the Boy Scout movement in 1908. The first senior scoutmaster here was Sgt. W.G. Perry who was assisted by Arthur Ponting. In the 1990s the troop was in great difficulties – it was unable to find premises of their own and failed to get a Lottery grant to build one. The acquisition of this building has given the Scouts a great fillip but they still have great difficulty in recruiting adults to support the activity.

To the left of St. Mary's Church, going down St Mary's Street and at the end of the terrace is:

6 St Mary's Street

This rubble stone terraced house has a date stone inscribed SIE 1732. This became a privately run lodging house for vagrants with two dormitories for males and females with a large sitting room downstairs. It was probably started as a hostel for workers building the railway kept by a bespectacled German known as Johnnie Fink (his real name was Finkenagel). There was reputed to be a post in the back garden to which bears from travelling menageries were chained. Mr. Fink would arrange for a German Band to attend the annual Mare and Colt Show at St Aldhelm Mead on 28th September. He emigrated to America before the Great War. Latterly the hostel was run by Mr. & Mrs. White who lived next door. It seems to have been closed just before World War II and a bed is said to have cost 2d. per night.

United Reform Church (Westport Congregational Church), St Mary's Street,
The Rev. S. Gawen, vicar of St Paul's, felt the Act of Uniformity 1662, intended to compel all clergymen to give their assent to the Book of Common Prayer, was unjust and along with 2,000 other ministers gave up his living. If he did not found the Westport Congregational Church he was its first minister but died in 1671. The church was Presbyterian from its formation until 1811 when most English Presbyterian Churches were renamed Congregational. The first chapel stood near the site of the present building in St Mary's Street. It was reached through an archway above which stood two cottages but this was demolished before the present building was erected in 1867 for £1,933. The original chapel was rebuilt in the 1788 and enlarged in 1828. During the 1930s the church sent missions to a daughter chapel in Corston. Unfortunately that chapel closed in July 1943. The Congregational Church merged with the Presbyterians from 5th October 1972 to form the United Reformed Church. During 1991 major alterations were made to the interior of the church, particularly on the ground floor.

A very important person associated with this site is;

Thomas Hobbes (1588-1679)
Hobbes was born prematurely on Good Friday when the Armada threatened the country. His home was a cottage in what is now St Mary's Street in front of the United Reform Church which was demolished in the middle of the 19th Century. Neither of his parents was distinguished; his father (also Thomas) was curate of Brokenborough. He was practically illiterate and a drunkard but a great card player. Such was his enthusiasm that he often fell asleep in church and had to be roused by his Clerk. There were also complaints that he failed to attend services. Unfortunately one day he struck and nearly killed

the vicar of Foxley who apparently simply wanted to talk about his son's education. He was forced to flee to London where he died in obscurity years later.

A modern view of the United Reform Church.

After attending a church school for two years Hobbes attended a grammar school in the Sheepfair [49 the Triangle]. The master, Robert Latimer was described by Aubrey as *'a good Grecian', who being a Bachelor (of Arts), not above 19, taught him and two or three ingeniose laddes after supper till 9, at his own house in Westport, where the broad place is, next door north from the Smyth's shop opposite the Three Cuppes, as I take it; by whom he so well profited that at 14 years old he went, a good scholar, to Magdalene Hall in Oxford and before he went did translate Euripidis Medea out of Greek into Latin iambiques.* Hobbes did not think much of Oxford but in 1607 obtained a Bachelor's degree. After that he became tutor to the teenaged (and married) William Cavendish and served three generations of the earls of Devonshire.

He travelled extensively throughout Europe with his aristocratic and royal patrons. He met Galileo in 1630. Hobbes was a vigorous proponent of scientific materialism and it was his regret that he was considered to be a philosopher rather than a scientist. He maintained a lively correspondence with other great men like Francis Bacon, Descartes, Fermat and Ben Jonson. *Leviathan* (1651) was his greatest work in which it is argued that as people are inherently selfish they need to be ruled by an absolute civil power to enforce public order. However his works often contained anti-monarchist sentiment and it is fortunate that he tutored the future Charles II in maths whilst in exile in France. The

King later granted him a pension of £100 per annum and hung Hobbes' portrait in the Royal Closet. Hobbes was proud of his birthplace and always used the style Thomas Hobbes of Malmesbury in his books. He died in 1679 and is buried in Ault Hucknall Church, Derbyshire.

21 St Mary's Street

This operated as the Barley Mow beer house from at least the middle of the 19th Century to 1922. Luce's Brewery owned it from 1871 until the Stroud Brewery took over in 1912. The auction particulars read; *Stone-built, containing: Public Kitchen, Beer Store, Sitting-room, 3 Bedrooms and Attic. Yard in rear with Coalhouse, washing Shed, Stable, Pigstye and underground Cellar.* In 1988 it became a dentists' surgery with a number of different partners since then.

You will see ahead the open space of Horsefair, another example of an 'out of town' market.

40 Horsefair

The Bath Arms opened its doors in these premises around 1850 and continued as a pub until 1957. It was then used as an off licence but in 1995 that closed and it became a private house.

Continue to the left along Burnham Road and just past the saddlers' on the right is:

1-5 Burnham Road, Old Police Station

Constables in Malmesbury were first recorded in the 1640s. Until 1839 law and order was the responsibility of Parish or Petty Constables who were appointed by Courts Leet and latterly by Magistrates in Quarter Sessions. They were unpaid, untrained and usually unwilling to undertake protracted investigations. Between 1729 and 1741 two constables each were appointed at borough sessions for Malmesbury and Westport. From 1753 another constable was added for the Abbey parish.

The agricultural and Chartist riots put an intolerable strain on this system. During November 1830 there were major agricultural disturbances throughout the Southwest in protest against poor wages and food price rises. Much damage was caused and machinery destroyed. The Wiltshire Yeomanry were called upon to assist on a number of occasions and were rewarded with the accolade of becoming a Royal regiment. The Municipal Corporations Act 1835 required Boroughs to set up Police forces. Counties pressed for similar powers which led to the County Police Act 1839. Wiltshire set up their force in the same year, the first outside London, appointing its Chief Constable that November. It was to comprise not less than 200 constables. Malmesbury Borough had a separate force from 1840 until 1887 when it was incorporated into the county force. In April 1840 two county officers were convicted and sent to prison for a month after an assault in Malmesbury.

The Malmesbury police less one PC, presumably out patrolling, at Gastons Lane in 1900. Sydney Kite is standing on the left. The building behind has been demolished and this area forms part of the carpark behind 1-5 Burnham Road.

The Superintendent in his cart which was bought from H. Willis of Devizes for £32. The cells and stable are behind.

Wiltshire police had a station at 1 Burnham Road (at that time called Horse Fair Road, Brokenborough parish) by 1854 which remained there until the mid 1950s. A sergeant lived in the station house, there were cottages for other members of the force next door with cells and stables at the rear. At the turn of the 20th Century Malmesbury formed one of nine Divisions of the Wiltshire Constabulary. There were subdivisions at Kemble (actually in Gloucestershire) and Sherston with eight other stations. The establishment of the town's contingent was one superintendent, three sergeants and eleven constables. The Superintendent then also was the Inspector of Contagious Diseases (Animals).

One of the constables was PC Sydney Kite. He was sent to check the pig licence for Backbridge Farm (which has since been demolished to make way for an expansion of the Dyson factory) around 1910. A rabbit was being cooked for lunch and he remarked that rabbit was too dry for his taste. The farmer, Sydney Melsome, assured him that his daughter's way of cooking rabbit ensured it was not dry and that he should come back when off duty to try one. He duly returned to obtain the proof, went on to marry the daughter and later became a farmer himself!

H. & C. Matthews, 7 Burnham Rd

Henry Matthews (b1860) served an apprenticeship as a carpentry joiner at Burton Hill House. Being an ambitious young man, at the earliest opportunity he began his own carpentry business. He rented a workshop and stable in Gastons Lane just outside the

Matthews premises in 2000. This photograph illustrates how overhead power and telephone cables blight many views in the town. The sign boasts of a motor hearse - the horses were called up for World War I and not replaced.

Borough boundary about 1880. His brother Charles (b1867), a wheelwright and a noted French polisher, also worked in the business for some time along with about a dozen others. Henry took on building work and built a number of houses in Minety, thinking nothing of the seven-mile journey there, pushing his cart each morning and evening. At the beginning of the 20th Century the firm built a number of elegant houses in Burnham Road and Charles lived at No. 11. Henry's son Stephen worked for the business for a while before emigrating to Australia. Stephen's son Charles took over the firm in the early 1950s and in turn his son Chris took charge until retiring in 2005. The first undertaking was done at the beginning of last century when there were six other carpenters in the town who did such work. In 1973 Chris decided to concentrate solely on being a funeral director.

Examine the terrace of houses on the south side of the road and you will realise that this is the back of the row. The Ordnance Survey shows a detached block of outside toilets that were demolished to widen the road. Retrace your steps to Horsefair and turn to the left down Foundry Road, continuing just past the junction with Shipton Hill (although this is still part of Foundry Road!) to:

Ratcliffe and Son, Foundry Road

Edwin Ratcliffe (1848-1916), the eldest son of a farmer from Bucklebury in Berkshire, opened the Westport Ironworks in 1870. The buildings to the north of the road incorpo-

Inside Ratcliffe's workshop in the early 20th Century. Otto Sealy (related to the family that ran the Triangle's weighbridge) is on the left, Bert Goddard in the centre and Edwin Ratcliffe on the right.

rate some early 19th Century farm buildings. Edwin had married the daughter of John Hedges who owned an iron foundry in Bucklebury and had presumably been apprenticed to him. Why he moved to Malmesbury is not clear but his brother Norman owned a chemist's at 19 High Street around the same time. Edwin designed and produced machinery for mills, breweries and factories as well as footbridges and hatches for the river authority. At first his workshop was powered by steam, later by gas until converted to electricity in 1940.

After the First World War the son, Edwin Norman (1892-1963) joined the business, which diversified into trades such as plumbing, the repair of steam traction engines and car hire. In its heyday the works employed 15 men. In 1940 Ratcliffe's fitted out the machinery for the Western Development Unit of Ekco [Cowbridge House]when they moved into Ponting's premises in the High Street. The original forge was last used in 1981 to make gates that were presented by the town of Tetbury to the Prince of Wales for Highgrove House. The founder's grandson Ted and great-grandson Mike now run the business, which concentrates on the repair and maintenance of lawnmowers and strimmers. Much of the original machinery is still in situ and this provides a strong incentive to take your lawnmower for a service here so that you have an excuse to see it!

Edwin Ratcliffe was probably a member of the Plymouth Brethren when he came to the town. He allowed them to use the first floor of a building he owned opposite his works as a chapel. He seems to have fallen out with them and before World War I it was a chapel no longer. During World War II the same premises were used as an Air Raid Wardens Post.

Go back to Shipton Hill and go down it. At the bottom junction you are flanked by a high brick wall on your right which is:

Westport Granary, Gloucester Road
First just look up to the 'Foundry Road' sign on the wall to your right. This is one of those inscribed "Jos$^{\underline{h}}$ Poole ^{Esq} Mayor 1890-91". This building was used by John Alexander's [Avon House] business, being next door to his son Walter's house. The warehouse was used by the Alexanders as agents for the West of England Sack Contractors Ltd. providing hessian sacks for use by farmers and millers. By 1895 the coal business had become the Malmesbury Coal Company (W. Alexander proprietor). The ownership of the company changed to Alexander & Co. around 1910 and H. Gladwin in 1937. After the last war the warehouse was used by Southern Electricity Board for many years.

Immediately in front of you is:

Stainsbridge House, Gloucester Road
In the middle of the 19th Century Thomas Chubb (1792-1869) [Priory] lived here. Capt. Richard Coote (1836-1875) bought the property for £600 in 1870 and rebuilt it the following year. Unfortunately he did not live long enough to fully enjoy his new resi-

Stainsbridge House whilst it was an hotel in 1964

dence, his memorial is just in front of you as you enter the Abbey. At the end of the 19th Century the widowed Mrs. Julia Clark started a girl's boarding school later called Stainsbridge College. This was taken over by Miss Geraldine Elder who was originally one of the Assistant Governesses until the 1930s. Then it became the residence of Frederick Ernest Smith (1844-1939), a retired solicitor. He had been in partnership with Walter Trevelyan Clark and had offices at 1 Market Cross which is now occupied by a travel agent. The solicitors continued to be run by Walter's family until his great grandsons, Donald Trevelyan and Godfrey Trevelyan broke up the business in the 1960s. They then traded separately for several years. During the Second World War Stainsbridge House was a National Childrens' Home and then in the 1950s it became a Hotel. In 1978 it was turned into a residential home for the elderly with accommodation for 29.

Stainsbridge House to Park Road

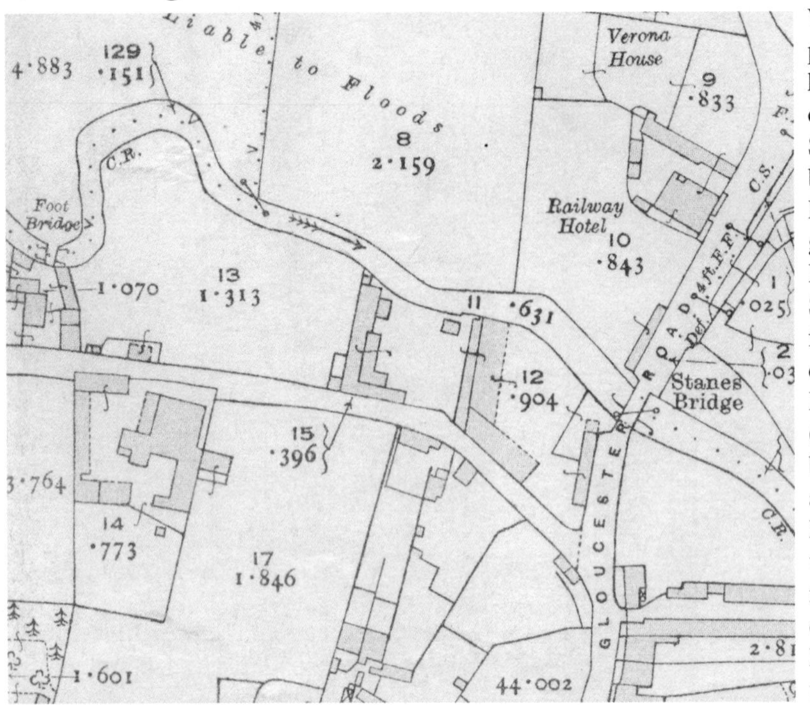

We now move to a part of the town that has changed markedly since 1923. Stanes Bridge has been widened, the Railway yard has gone and the Railway Hotel replaced by Somerfield's. The forage yard on the corner of Gloucester Road and Park Road (marked 12 with .904 below on the map) and the Bacon Factory (number 14 with .775 underneath) have both disappeared with houses built where they were. Walk down the hill to the first small roundabout. Opposite a new group of houses is on the site of a turnpike cottage on the road to Tetbury. It was later owned by Joe Moore who in addition to owning the Old Bell ran a forage business at Stainsbridge Mill. Jack Willis bought the firm in 1936 when the name changed to Moore & Willis until he sold out to Rawlings & Phillips of Calne. Within a few years they were taken over and the site was sold to Athelstan Garage which traded from here for 30 years.

Stainsbridge

Stainsbridge (a corruption of Theyn's Bridge, derived from William le Theyn who held an estate at Brokenborough in the 13th Century) is one of 5 bridges giving access to Malmesbury. Before leaving look at the bridge, from the east you can see that it is a prefabricated concrete span resting on the stone arches of the old bridge. That could only take one-way traffic until modernised in 1960. There were high walls abutting the bridge and on 15th July 1933 a young girl named Margaret Gleed broke free from her sister into the path of a Western National bus on its way to Stroud which struck and killed her.

To the north east of the bridge at the present stands;

Fire Station

Although the town had a Fire Engine for some time (one built around 1700 and last used in 1845 at Burton Hill House is in the Museum), it was not until 1851 that the Fire Brigade was established. At the outset it was financed mainly by public subscription. It started off with a 5 inch pump with 80 feet of hose to draw water from the river or wells and 12 paid part time staff. In the early years about two fires were attended annually and charges were made for their services. The first Fire Station was probably in Ingram Street around 1886.

By 1900 the Brigade had a horse-drawn Merryweather hand pump based in a Station at the Stoneyard, Horsefair (now Stan Steven's workshop in Katifer Lane) and the alarm was raised by the church bells. The Superintendent was the Borough Surveyor. By this time the Borough Council provided the finance and attendance to fires in the Borough was free but there was a scale of charges for elsewhere. On 21st July that year the bill for attending a fire at Lodge Farm, Little Somerford was:

Engine	£3 3s. 0d.
Horse Hire	£2 2s. 0d.
Superintendent	£1 1s. 0d.
Engineer and Hoseman, 15hrs @ 1/3d. per hour	£1 17s. 6d.
10 firemen, 15hrs @ 1s. per man hour	£7 10s. 0d.
13 supernumeraries @ 7s. 6d. each	£4 17s. 6d.
Total	£20 11s. 0d.

In that December the Borough Fire Brigade Committee found the Brigade in good order but a year later the situation had changed dramatically and they decided to disband it and form a new Brigade. In 1907 the Station moved to the Town Hall in Cross Hayes. At this time the alarm was the Silk Mill siren. Horses were then provided by Duck's Brewery [32 Cross Hayes] which kept them in stables in Cross Hayes Lane, but later the Borough Council had two horses that normally pulled the ash cart. However sometimes when the alarm sounded someone had to run and catch horses loose in a meadow by the river in Holloway. There were arrangements to use other horses when the usual team was unavailable and one such agreement was made with Adye and Son [52 High Street]. A new horse-drawn Merryweather 'Gem' steam pump was bought in 1920.

The 'King Athelstan' Dennis appliance with the Merryweather steamer behind it on the right. The photograph is taken at Burton Hill House with what is now the Chapel in the background. The Mayor, James Jones, is in the driver's seat and next to him is Captain Scott MacKirdy. The Fire Captain Egbert ('Eggy') Edwards is the portly gent on the right. The Mayor's chain probably indicates this was taken on 10th October 1925.

Sopworth House after the fire. Originally the Rectory (note the Church closeby), and subsequently much extended. The fire was thought to have been started by clothes drying in front of the fire in the children's nursery. The Stanleys were very wealthy and they rebuilt the house with some modifications. They sold the house around 1950 and it was later split into 3 separate residences, now called Sopworth Manor.

10th October 1925 saw a great change with the purchase of a petrol driven Dennis 35hp, 250/300 gallon light turbine with ladder, christened King Athelstan. The purchase price of 1,000 guineas was raised by public subscription, as it was for all of the appliances then. In March 1926 the Brigade was embarrassed by a major fire at Sopworth that got out of control. A defective flue in the nursery of Sopworth House caught light during the night. The owners, Colonel and Mrs. Stanley tried to raise the alarm by telephone but were unable to get any response. Eventually a Police Constable in Luckington saw the glow of the fire on the horizon. He got a lift to the Police Station in Sherston. From there he was able to phone the Police in Malmesbury who called Edgar Basevi, the town's photographer, who lived at 32 Gloucester Street. He woke his neighbour Bill Paginton, a fireman whose job was to alert the Fire Captain, Egbert Edwards (b1879) who lived at 27 Holloway. The fire engine was on its way within 6 minutes and arrived in Sopworth 18 minutes later. By the time it arrived the fire had been burning for at least 2½ hours and the Chippenham Brigade were already there. Councillors at the Borough Council meeting on 2 April called on the Postmaster General to carry out a full enquiry. The reason for the debacle was because the telephonist on duty at Malmesbury's exchange, Reg Wakefield, was asleep.

Shortly afterwards Capt. Scott Mackirdy [Abbey House] promoted a mutual aid scheme between a number of communities bounded by Tetbury and Corsham in the west, Marlborough in the east and Trowbridge and Devizes in the south with Chippenham at the centre which also housed the control room. Between them they could call upon 10 motor pumps, two trailer pumps and many other appliances. Malmesbury was part of the West Midlands District of the National Fire Brigades Association and entered their competitions each year. The District comprised 61 authorities and the brigade was pleased to win a trophy in July 1927 at Banbury.

Councillor Scott Mackirdy presented a Studebaker ambulance to the Borough on 20th November 1927. Before World War II it cost users 10d. per mile with a minimum of 5s., described in Riddick's Directories *which charge merely represents the actual cost of running*. During 1928 a new electric alarm system with a bell in each fireman's home was installed. It took an average of 4½ minutes to call the crew out. Malmesbury was justifiably proud of its firemen and installed a prominent sign on each of their houses.

The Fire Brigades Act 1938 prepared the service for war although little changed locally. The Rural District Council [10 High Street] should have become the local Fire Authority but they did not disturb the arrangement whereby the Borough Council administered the Brigade, with both Councils contributing to the cost and sometimes complaining about their share. A small trailer pump was acquired which was towed by the Chief Officer's car.

At the end of the war the King Athelstan appliance reached the end of its life. It was replaced by an Austin Hose Reel Tender (HRT) with trailer pump, a type commonly used during the war and this lasted until the early 1960s. It was joined by a similar auxiliary towing vehicle (ATV) that could tow the pump and carry other equipment such as extra hose reels. These were the two appliances when, following the Fire Services Act 1947, the Brigade became the responsibility of Wiltshire County Council.

The Studebaker ambulance also expired during the war. A requisitioned Rolls Royce was converted but was returned to its owner when the war ended. A Ford V8 was used for a short while until an ex Army Austin with an open front was obtained. This ambulance, based in Cross Hayes at the back of the George Hotel, was taken over by the County

The Austin Hose Reel Tender (HRT) with trailer pump in the Cross Hayes. This was a common wartime appliance mounted on a shortened military Austin K2 chassis. Just behind the passenger is an aperture containing one of two small hoses that could be used on arrival using water from a tank on board before the pump was set up .

Council in 1948.

The Fire Station in the Town Hall caused problems due to the narrowness of the entrance and exit. The engine was able to drive through from the yard behind which was also used for exercises. In 1962 a small Dennis F8 appliance built in 1953 with a Rolls Royce engine moved here from Calne. This vehicle, registration number JMW 424, is now preserved in the Atwell-Wilson Museum at Calne. It remained here until the Station moved to its present building in the Old Station Yard during 1969.

Since then there have been regular changes of equipment, for example, in 1969 a Bedford tender, 1979 a Dodge tender, and so on. The fire engine in 2004 is the prototype Dennis Sabre Water Tender Ladder Rescue Appliance. This was designed by a consortium of five brigades and has more equipment than production models including an exhaust brake, winch, cutting and lifting gear. Retained or part-time fire fighters are wholly responsible for this station. They are summoned by the alarm which is raised by a signal from the new combined service control room in Devizes. This travels along one of two telephone lines or a microwave link to activate the radio transmitter in the station that sets off each fire fighter's bleeper if it is within range.

Somerfield Supermarket, 120 Gloucester Road

The Railway Hotel opened here in 1880, shortly after the railway and was directly opposite the station. George Poole [Burnham House] became the licensee in 1881 for a few years. The pub was renamed the Flying Monk in 1964 following the closure of the

The Railway Hotel around 1900. There were a number of outbuildings to the right and rear.

railway. Demolished in the 1980s to make way for the Gateway store, the development was delayed several years apparently because the land belonged to British Rail rather than the brewery which had sold it. This probably was a result of the Wilts and Gloucestershire Railway scheme.

There is a small road to the left of the supermarket which leads to the Flying Monk playing field, the home of:

Malmesbury Victoria Football Club

Malmesbury Town Football Club was formed around 1897. By 1910 Colonel Charles Miles of Burton Hill House provided financial support. During the 1920s and 30s matches were played here at the Railway Hotel, Douglas Field (near Backbridge Farm where Dyson is now), Quobwell Farm on Tetbury Road and the Suffolk Arms (the site of which is now a small housing development on Tetbury Hill). The Treasurer reported to the Annual General Meeting in the White Lion on 9th June 1936 that the club was running at a loss. Attendances were poor, new officers could not be found and the club was wound up. Around 1947 Jock Patterson, a demon centre forward who later scored 8 goals in one game, helped to reform the club. To generate cash they formed the Skittles League in 1949 – this has now turned into a thriving organisation in its own right with nearly 100 teams participating. In the late 1960s the football club's name was changed to Malmesbury United. In 1976 the fixtures of Swindon Victoria were taken over and the name was changed again. Since the reformation of the club matches have been played at a variety of locations including St. Aldhelm's Mead, Brokenborough Hill, Corston, Corn Gastons before the school was built and later on that school's playing field. The present ground was used for post war livestock markets until 1966 and the club moved here in the 1970s. However when the pub was demolished in 1984/6 a pitch at Seagry was used. Many trophies have been won over the years but the club was the first to win both the 1st and 2nd Divisions of the Wiltshire League in 1972/3 and were runners up in Division I in both 1976/7 and 1995/6. The first team now plays in the Hellenic League which has led to the ground being fenced and floodlighting being installed.

Malmesbury Amateur Boxing Club

During the 1920s Charles Jones (1898-1975) organised fights in the Town Hall. He had been sent out to Canada in 1912 and served as a Mountie before he ran away to war. When the war ended he came to Malmesbury and worked for Dore Fielder & Company the auctioneers who at that time owned the lease of the Town Hall. He competed successfully as a heavy-weight and organised many tournaments. This led to a club being formed but it faded away before World War II. The club was revived in the late 1940s by Arthur Rogers. Bouts were held in the Town Hall and in a marquee erected in a field up the 'four and twenty steps' – just past Avon Mill. Again enthusiasm waned after a few years. Eric Lewis, an ex boxer, reformed the club in 1977. Originally they trained in the primary school gym but in 1980 moved to the Cartmell Centre in Ingram Street. When the British Legion wanted to sell those premises the club leased some land at the football field from the Town Council and built their own gym there. The club has an enviable record and is probably the best in the South West with youngsters getting to the last stages of many national competitions.

Athelstan Players

During the 1930s a group of thespians, foremost of whom was Bernard Basevi, laid on plays mainly for their own amusement. During the war more public performances were arranged to provide money for the hospital. When Bernard Basevi died Blithe Spirit was in rehearsal and it was only after much heart searching that the production went ahead. In those early years youngsters were not allowed to attend unless there was need for a child actor. In their 50th year the group built a studio by the football field at the rear of Somerfields. Their proud boast is that unlike the Windmill they never close!

In the 1930s the Flitch Trial was an important Carnival event. A married couple had to agree not to quarrel for a year. A trial would be held to see if they deserved the flitch (a side of bacon). This is the August 1939 trial of Mr. & Mrs. Woodward.

Cross the river by the pedestrian bridge into the industrial estate:

Park Road Industrial Estate (Milk Factory)

With the rich farming area all around the town it used to be renowned for agricultural products. A milk processing factory opened here in February 1919. Initially owned by Wiltshire Farmers Ltd. the name changed the following year to Wilts and Somerset Farmers Ltd. Milk was sterilised using a large coal fired boiler and the finished product was despatched to London by rail. At this time churns were carried by a De Dion lorry made in France. Wiltshire Creameries Ltd. took the business over and used the first bulk road tanker in Wiltshire which from 1931 was provided by Bulwark Transport of

A Sentinel steam lorry and two Lacre lorries of Wiltshire Farmers Ltd. being loaded with milk churns.

Chippenham. The railway continued to be used by individual farmers but it lost valuable traffic.

Cheese was made once a year when there was a surplus of milk, normally in early summer. United Dairies took over the business and as part of their reorganisation closed

Looking east from the Bacon Factory along Park Road to the old Milk Factory when it was owned by the Council in 1964.

these premises in 1938. Two of the staff moved to the larger depot at Wootton Bassett which shut in 2000. The Borough Council wanted to use the well here as a new source for the town's water supply and bought the Malmesbury factory in 1940. The quality and reliability of the supply from Conygre Mead had been in question for some time and this new source helped to overcome these difficulties. The site was used by the military as a laundry during the war and afterwards as a Council Depot. In 1986 it was converted into the present small industrial estate, having been taken over by the District Council in the 1974 local government changes.

Turn right into Park Road until you see on the left:

Willow View Close (Bacon Factory)
This was site for the first such factory in Wiltshire which was opened in 1877 by Adye and Hinwood Ltd. The principals were Alfred Adye [52 High Street] who raised the capital by selling that business to his brother Albert and Thomas Lot Hinwood [37/39 High Street]. The railway station just a few hundred yards away was well placed for the transportation of produce. To enable increased production this was one of the first plants to have refrigeration just after the Great War and for the next 20 years much was exported. After World War II up to 500 pigs were processed every week but within a few years the number shrank to around 200. The factory finally closed in 1964 and the company wound up the next year. Eventually houses were built to form Willow View Close and the rubble from the demolition was dumped in the 'factory field' across Park Road so that bungalows could be built along the riverbank.

The Bacon Factory in 1964 just after it had closed. The photograph has been taken from the north side of the road - where there is a row of bungalows now.

Further along the road on the righthand side is:

Park Road to Burnham House

In the 1920s this was out in the country. Park Road is a cart track (from the top left to the middle of the map on the right). There is a timber yard and one house (the Willows) north of it. Lanes now called St Aldhelms Road and Old Alexander Road have been laid out with fences on either side, but these appear to be blocked at the junction with Park Road. Note the dotted line showing the Borough boundary. The abattoir was built in the field marked 25^l & ·699.

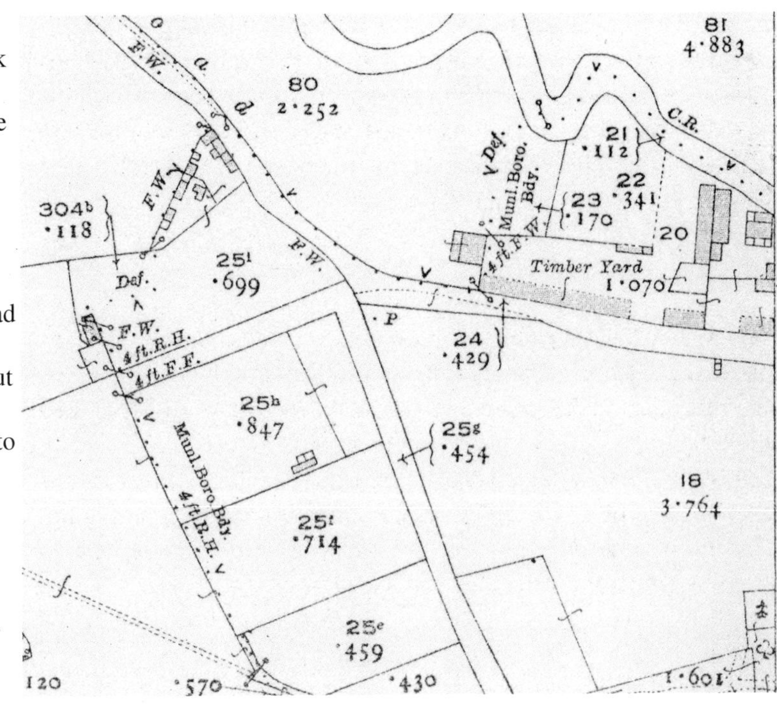

Park Mead

On the accompanying map you will see that in the 1920s there was a timber yard on this site. Just after the Second World War Athelstan Coaches had a garage at the top of Silver Street [32 Cross Hayes] but by the 1960s they had moved here. As well as running excursions and providing transport for many local societies including taking children to Ecko's Christmas Parties [Cowbridge House], they ran some bus services particularly one to Cirencester. With bus deregulation the main local operators Bristol Omnibus and Western National were broken up and new bus routes were developed. Athelstan Coaches was taken over by Overland and County in 1986 but unfortunately that company went into liquidation a few years later.

Continue along Park Road until you reach a cross roads and to the right is:

Park Close

George Frederick Day set up a butcher's shop around 1911 at 2 Market Cross, still used by Walkers Butchers. He also built an abattoir in Park Road (now Park Close) just inside the Borough boundary in the 1920s. This was run by him and his son Arthur for 30 years. In 1953 V & G Newman, farming brothers from Lea, took over, expanded and finally bought it. In the 1970s new premises were built to cope with the increasing trade. It closed in 1998 after the imposition of stringent hygiene regulations. Just a couple of

The abattoir just after closure. Houses now cover the whole site and there is much less greenery.

months before closure it brought worldwide fame to Malmesbury when two Tamworth pigs escaped. They were nicknamed Butch and Sundance or the Tamworth Two. They were at large for a week whilst scores of journalists pursued them. When recaptured they were bought by the Daily Mail and sent to an animal sanctuary.

Go up St. Aldhelm Road to the left and at the top of the hill is:

Burnham House, Burnham Road.

This house was built towards the end of the 19th Century by Fred Poole (1866-1907), one of famous brothers who ran Myrioramas. Their grandfather Richard Poole, a fuller of cloth moved to Malmesbury before 1841 and seems to have been employed at Avon Mill as he lived in the Lower High Street. He had three sons John (1817-1889), Charles (1821-1877) and George Walter (1828-1877). Moses Gompertz started touring the country with 'Panoramas' of colourful events like Arctic expeditions, battles and fires which he called Myrioramas. Charles and George joined his company as musicians until 1863 when in partnership with Anthony Young they took the business over. They developed the shows which involved scenery painted on canvas rolls that moved from a reel on one side of the stage to another on the opposite side as the story progressed. This was accompanied by music and fireworks with the whole illuminated by special lighting effects powered by gas! John had five sons Joseph (1847-1906), George (1849-1929), Henry (1850-1925), Charles (1858-1918) and Fred. Joseph joined his uncles in 1865 and built Verona House in Tetbury Hill (now the offices of Persimmon Homes Wessex Ltd). Next door to Verona is the large building that was later used as a school gymnasium and is now the Cartmell Youth Centre. Its original purpose was for Joseph's artists to paint the scenery. Joseph became Mayor in 1890. Fred began work with Joseph in 1878 but in

1896 formed a partnership with Henry. After Fred died his widow moved away from the town.

Burnham House was occupied by a number of people until 'Nipper' Constance moved here in 1949. He developed his veterinary practice [George Vets] here until he left Malmesbury in 1964. After 1968 the house was unoccupied. Councillor Jim Owen of the Town Council felt that it would make a good facility for local old folk and persuaded the County Council to buy it in 1971. Unfortunately they could not find the capital to convert it so the property was plagued by vandals and boarded up. In 1977 it was finally opened as a day centre for the elderly. Jim Owen raised money to furnish it and arranged for pupils from the Corn Gastons school to decorate it. It was such a success that in 1981 the County Council and Health Authority shared the cost of £442,000 to add residential facilities for 50 people. Some 40 to 45 staff are employed in the home. The project has also received support from charities. In 1977 Mr. C.H. Barnes, a former railway worker, left money in trust for the project and later the estate of a resident, Mrs. Hale, was added to it. This fund paid £31,500 to expand the day care areas of the sitting room and dining room during 1995. The Malmesbury Community Trust now administers this charity. The County Council agreed to sell this property along with nine other homes for older people to Coverage Care Ltd. in the summer of 1999 but public opinion has caused them to reconsider and the deal fell through. However it was later sold to the Order of St. John.

Burnham House taken in 1964. It has been extended to be several times its original size.

Burnham House to Foxley Road

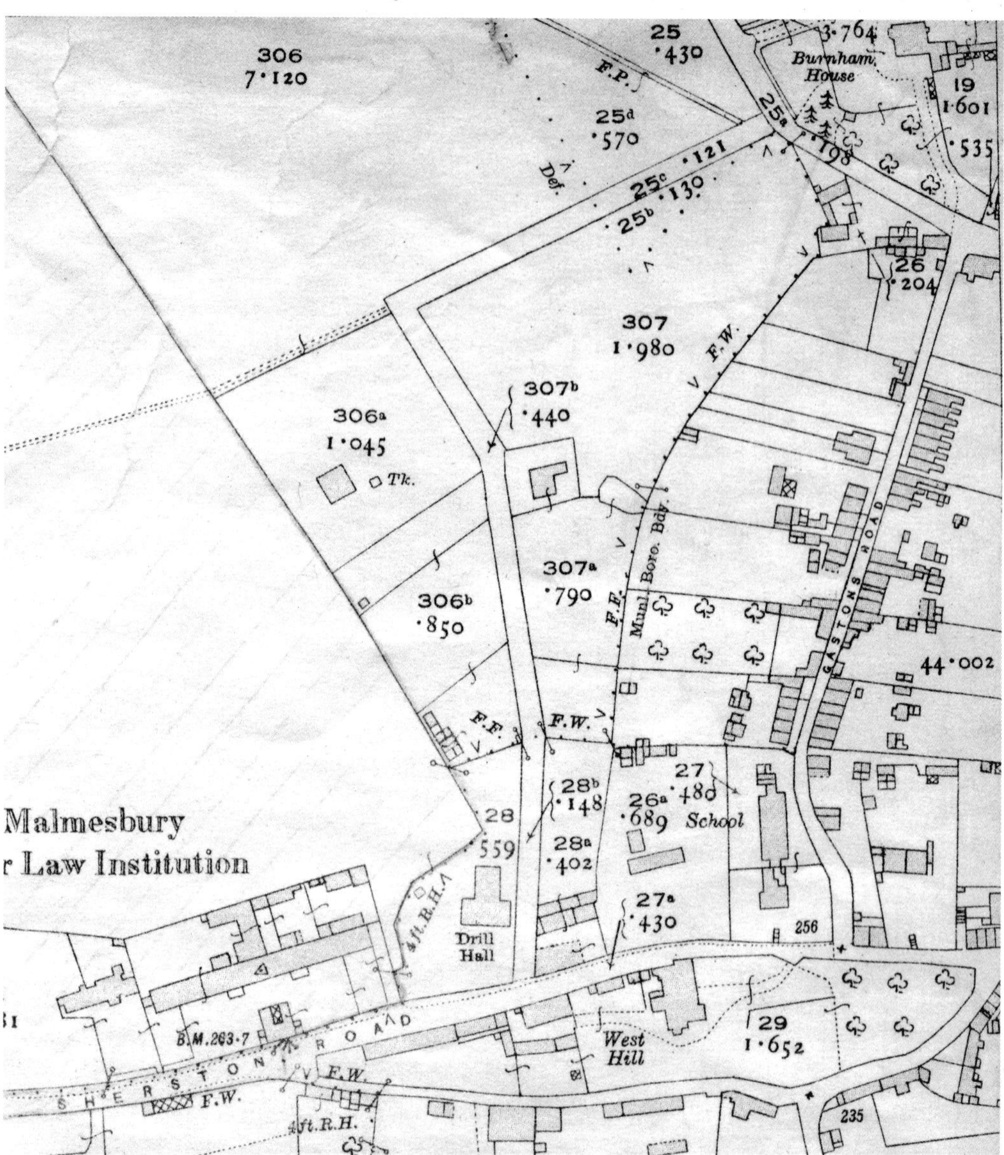

This area has completely changed. Pool Gastons and Bremilham Roads were laid out although only Bremilham House had been built. There are now more houses at the north end of Gastons Road with a few other new buildings further down the road. Now the Workhouse has been demolished, being replaced by houses and other new properties have been built along Sherston Road and Dark Lane.

Turn down Pool Gastons Road and on the right hand side are what used to be:

Council Houses

In 1931 the Borough Council bought land around Pool Gastons and began to build about 60 council houses in Pool Gastons Road and Athelstan Road. These houses were originally lit by gas and had no electricity supply. This development was extended over 10 years after 1946 when another 125 council houses were built in Alexander Road, Avon Road, Hobbes Close and Corn Gastons. In the late 1950s and early 1960s 40 more were put up in Newnton Grove.

The Rural District Council began developing the Parklands Estate in 1958 and built 55 council houses. In the late 1960s 84 more houses, bungalows and sheltered homes were added. The same decade saw around 100 private houses being erected in White Lion Park. In 1972 the Workhouse in Bristol Road was demolished and 27 council houses were built in Bremilham Rise.

Local councils built most new houses before the 1970s but with increasing personal wealth central government decided that the majority of future projects would be private. After 1979 council houses were offered to tenants at heavily discounted prices and many Malmesbury residents have taken advantage of this. North Wiltshire District Council transferred their remaining housing stock to North Wiltshire Housing Association Ltd. on 11th December 1995. This company was renamed Westlea Housing Association in June 1999.

More recent expansion of the town has taken place to the north and south. In the late 1980s Persimmon Homes completed an estate of over 300 homes at Reeds Farm and at the time of writing look likely to add another 150 on the old school site at Filands. Earlier around 50 houses were erected north of Burton Hill House.

At the end of the road you can glimpse:

Malmesbury Comprehensive School

During the 19th Century a number of Elementary Schools [Library and St Aldhelm's Church] were opened that catered for children up to the age of 14. The first secondary school for children aged between 8 and 14 was the Technical School which opened in the back of the Council Chamber, Silver Street in September 1896. The premises were described as *three classrooms approached by a long narrow passageway; a small chemical laboratory, a shed for practical work and a caretaker's room made of corrugated iron and matchboard registering 81°F when inspected.* To begin with there were only five scholars with two teachers, Mr. Cameron and Mr. Eatell, covering a wide syllabus with the expected Arithmetic, English, History, Latin etc. but also including subjects such as Agriculture, Bookkeeping, Euclid and Land Surveying. Other 'Sub-Centres' for learning and examinations were set up in many surrounding villages. The Executive Committee chaired by the Earl of Suffolk arranged for pioneer lectures to be held in the villages *in order that an interest in the subjects of Instruction may be awakened.* The school was soon popular and new premises for up to 75 scholars were opened

The new school building on Tetbury Hill that opened in 1903, pictured when the Grammar School moved again in 1964.

for classes on 7th January 1903 at the foot of Tetbury Hill at a cost of £5,192. In order to contribute towards this the Rural District Council agreed to levy a rate of $^{3}/_{8}$d. in £1. The description of this building was *two classrooms on the ground floor, a cookery kitchen, woodwork shop, Headmaster's and Mistress' room, boys' and girls' cloakroom and offices. On the first floor another classroom, an Art room, two laboratories and a lecture theatre*.

Not long after this, Wiltshire County Council took over responsibility for education and the school was renamed the Malmesbury and District County Secondary School. Even though this was the official title it was generally known as the 'grammar school' although it did not become one until 1954! Parents were required to commit to keep their children here until age 16, although the legal obligation for the school leaving age under the Education Act 1918 was 14. In 1921 Verona House was bought to provide accommodation for the Headmaster and space to allow the school to expand to 120 pupils. The County threatened to close the school in 1935 but, despite this, expansion took place in the late 1930s and 1944. Riddick's (a family of stationers and printers that operated from 15 High Street from the middle of the 19th Century until 1977) Year Books during the late 1930s contained the following information:

The Malmesbury and District County Secondary School - Headmaster, Mr. K. Willmore, B.SC.., B.COM. (B.A.). Staff, Miss M. M. Browne, M.A., Miss E. M. Bevan, B.A., Miss R. M. Wise, B.A, Miss M. E. Oatley, Mr. J. J. Chipchase, B.SC.., Mr. J. W. Davies, B.A.., Mr. S. L. Hockey, M.A.., Mr. G. W. Tracy. Art Master, Mr. A. F. Hayward.

The School, established in 1903 as a Secondary School for boys and girls, is maintained by the Wiltshire County Council. It is administered by a body of 21 Governors. Chairman of the Governors, Alderman J. A. Jones; secretary to the Governors, Mr. C. Bradshaw, 10, High Street, Malmesbury.

Boys and girls whose parents wish them to enter the school should see that they sit for the County Examination held in the early part of the year. On the results of this examination, supplemented by an oral test or interview, will be awarded a number of County Junior Scholarships carrying complete exemption from school fees. Other children who reach a sufficient standard in the examination will be admitted at fees of three, six, nine or twelve guineas a year according to the income and financial responsibilities of their parents. Parents are required to sign an agreement promising to keep the pupil at school until July of the year in which he (or she) attains the age of sixteen

A number of maintenance allowances are awarded from time to time by:—

(a) The Trustees of the Elizabeth Hodge's Charity.

(b) The Trustees of the Michael Week's Charity [Almshouses].

(c) The Capital Burgesses of Malmesbury.

(d)) The Trustees of the Warner Bequest.

Elizabeth Hodges in her will of 1723 gave £30 per year to schools in Malmesbury and in 1730 this was used for a school for 15 boys. This school was amalgamated with the Westport National School in 1869 and the fund is now administered by local trustees. The arrival of evacuees at the beginning of World War II created a shortage of teachers and one of the original teachers, Mr. Eatell, returned at the age of 86! In 1944 secondary education became free.

A Practical Instruction Centre was opened at Corn Gastons in 1950 to teach cookery and

The view of Bremilham Secondary Modern School at Corn Gastons from the entrance at Pool Gastons Road in the 1960s.

The 'new' Grammar School under construction at Filands in 1964.

woodwork. This was used by pupils from the two National Schools. However it was not until 1954 that the Bremilham Secondary Modern School was opened in a new building at Corn Gastons. This started with 30 teachers and 450 pupils. At the same time the Secondary School became the Grammar School and pupils had to pass the dreaded Eleven Plus examination to gain entry. This School outgrew its premises and in 1964 move to a new site at the junction of Tetbury Hill and Filands. The Cross Hayes Primary School was able to move onto the vacated site.

Whilst the benefits of the new site were just being enjoyed, the Labour government implemented the Robbins Report which recommended comprehensive schooling. In 1971 both secondary schools were combined into the Malmesbury School. The Lower School (junior scholars) was at Filands and the Upper School at Corn Gastons. In the late 1990s the cost resulting from the school being on two sites led to the decision to move onto one site at Corn Gastons. This was financed through the Private Finance Initiative, in other words without the help of state funds. Contractors put up the buildings necessary and became leasehold owners of the buildings with the County Council paying rent. This project, combined with others at Chippenham and Wootton Bassett, obtained Government approval at the end of 1998 and was completed in 2001.

Turn left along Bremilham Road and on the brow of the hill look at:

The Activity Zone Leisure Centre and Swimming Pool, Bremilham Road
Until September 2003 there was an open air swimming pool in Alexander Road. This was planned before the Second World War with Bernard Basevi spearheading the effort to get it built. After the war proceeds from Carnivals helped to raise the funds. It was built at the rear of Alexander Road beside a footpath that led from the Horsefair to allotments at White Lion Park and was finally opened in 1961. The total cost of £12,500 was shared between the Borough Council and public donations. The Chamber of Commerce raised £4,300 from a series of lotteries that they organised. In 1998 an anonymous donor promised £300,000 towards a new indoor pool and a National Lottery grant was obtained to provide further finance. This new facility was built next to the Activity Zone. The first Lottery application was rejected because the plan was thought to be too grandiose and a more modest version was constructed with for example only a small area for spectators to stand in. The planning of the Activity Zone was more straightforward and construction began in June 1998. Half of the cost of more than £2.7M was financed by a grant from the National Lottery Awards Panel with North Wiltshire District Council contributing £785,000. Providing facilities for many indoor sports, it opened on 19th June 1999.

At the end of the road pause at:

Holford Rise

The western side of Bremilham Road close to the junction with Bristol Road was the site of a Drill Hall that opened on 4th January 1912. In modern times the first militia unit in the town was a Company that met at the White Lion in the middle of the 18th Century. Another war with the French led to a troop of the Wiltshire Yeomanry being formed here in 1794. This unit carried on until the Second World War. In 1859 another fear of invasion by the French caused the War Office to ask Lord Lieutenants to form new Rifle Volunteers. Malmesbury was the second town in Wiltshire to heed this call to arms.

Other places where there were Drill Halls include behind 85 High Street believed to have been used by the Yeomanry until the 1930s, by the water tower at Abbey House which housed the Rifle Volunteers, the warehouse behind 32 Cross Hayes for a platoon of 4th Bn. Wiltshire Regiment before World War II and the present 1930s building on Tetbury Hill now used by 992 Squadron Air Training Corps. This Bristol Road site was first used by the Ammunition Column of 3rd Wessex Brigade, Royal Field Artillery that was formed from the Company of Rifle Volunteers in 1908 when the Territorial Force came into existence. The stables were across the road where Custom Transformers now are. This unit does not appear to have been reactivated after the First World War.

In 1923 this Drill Hall was bought by Alfred Ernest Adye (b1869) son of Alfred [Willow View Close] who turned it into a motor garage. In 1930 he passed it on to his sons Reginald Victor (1901-1962) and Norman Ernest (1905-1983) who entered into a partnership. Reg ran the garage whilst Norman opened a Radio Shop at 6 High Street.

Adye's Garage in the 1960s. In the centre is the old Drill Hall used as workshops. The showroom to the left was the wooden structure used as the Electric Picturedrome behind 92 High Street that was brought here after the Athelstan Cinema had been built.

The motor dealership was expanded in 1932 when the Gig House, Oxford Street was bought – these premises were sold in 1948. The radio business moved to Bristol Road in the 1960s but moved to 57 Gloucester Road until that shop closed in 1996. The garage was sold in 1982 and the drill hall demolished soon afterwards.

Turn to the right and go as far as the pathway on the right:

Bremilham Rise

This was the site of the Workhouse. The Poor Law Amendment Act 1834 promoted fundamental changes in local administration although its purpose was simply to provide a new system of poor law relief. Previously this had been the responsibility of individual parishes and the standard of care varied. Under the new law, parishes were gathered into Unions and the Malmesbury Union was formed in 1835 which comprised - Abbey (Malmesbury), Alderton, Brinkworth, Brokenborough, Charlton, Crudwell, Dauntsey, Easton Grey, Foxley, Garsdon, Great Somerford, Hankerton, Hullavington, Lea and Cleverton, Little Somerford, Luckington, Malmesbury St Paul Within, Malmesbury St Paul Without, Minety, Norton, Oaksey, Sherston, Sopworth and Westport St Mary Within. Malmesbury had its first workhouse in what was later called Tower House. The new Board of Guardians met for the first time on 5th December 1835, but it was not until September of the following year that they decided to replace the four workhouses at Minety, Malmesbury, Crudwell and Sherston here just outside the Borough's boundary in Brokenborough. It was completed in 1838 and cost £2,800.

The conditions were deliberately unattractive with married couples being separated. Up

This view of the Workhouse from across the river valley emphasises its size - the premises of Custom Transformers is on the right. More houses have been built in the foreground along Dark Lane and Bristol Road.

to 230 inmates could be accommodated. Work had to be done to earn one's keep and typical tasks were breaking stones for use on the roads (there was a quarry opposite) or chopping up old railway sleepers into firewood that was then sold in the area. There was a separate Hospital building which was built in 1850/1 at a cost of £630. A large bell rang at 6.45 am, 8 am (for breakfast), 12 noon (dinner), 5 pm (tea), and 7.45 pm (supper). The workhouse had its own covered hearse that was used to take back the bodies of inmates who died to the parish from which they came for a pauper's burial. Sydney Kite from Park Lane Farm provided the horse for these journeys.

When the County Council took over the responsibility for poor relief on 1st April 1930, Malmesbury's Workhouse was an early casualty and closed in 1933. It was bought by the Borough Council for £400 which between 1936 and 1938 turned it into dwellings with a rent lower than other council houses. In 1972 it was demolished and 27 council houses were built on the site. The main building overlooked the road where Bremilham Rise now is. The only reminder is the stone wall to the west of Holford Rise, and a few feet up the pathway you can see the outline of the Porter's Gate.

Now retrace your steps along Bristol Road to the narrow brow of the hill at the junction of Crab Tree Close and to the right is:

Westhill House

This area was originally an isolated small pocket of the parish of Bremilham, but became part of Westport St. Mary in 1884. It seems that this arrangement arose because the Holford family owned this land and were Lords of the Manor. The house here was known as The Light, which may be an ironic contrast to Dark Lane (apparently so called due to having high ground to its north with shrubs and trees overshadowing it). A house was on the site from before 1793 but it was greatly enlarged at the end of the 19th Century. Around 1900 when the name of the house changed, a wealthy gentleman called John Martin lived here. He was married with 2 sons and a daughter with the household looked after by 10 servants! After the First World War, Isaac Beak (1856-1931) owned the house. His son Ronald (1891-1937) ran a corn chandler's from the shed opposite Bremilham Road. Ronald's widow Florence (1896-1987) moved his business which then sold seeds to 40 High Street. After Isaac's death his daughters ran a kindergarten at Westhill in the late 1930s for the Parents National Education Union. Presumably his widow (Elizabeth 1858-1947) was unable to afford such large premises and in 1939 she sold it to John Mott [St. Michael's Court]. The property comprised all of the land bounded by Bristol Road, Dark Lane and Foxley Road.

During the Second World War a tennis court was built (Chalcourt now stands on this) as well as a swimming pool (where the Pines is now). Wartime shortages of materials like concrete made this construction difficult. After the war at the eastern end of the site, some land was sold to the County Council to widen the roads. In Bristol Road a footway was added on the south side and Foxley Road was considerably widened at the junction. Originally the boundary wall was roughly where the white line is in the middle of the road! Mrs Langley purchased the house in 1962 and converted it to a Nursing Home. Dr and Mrs Coleman took this over in 1965. This was closed due to some difficulties in the late 1980s. Dr David Jackson and originally 3 partners reopened the New Westhill Nursing Home in 1989. Just 10 years later, due to the need to upgrade facilities, it was no longer economically viable and this well-used local amenity closed. The following year the building was converted into 3 town houses.

At the junction with Gastons Road above you to the left is:

National Boys' School

In the 1850s the Boys' School in the Guildhall needed larger premises and the Church was grateful to be given land in Crab Tree Close - you will see that this name has been reused for the new housing on the brow of the hill - by Robert Stayner Holford (1808-1892) of Westonbirt who is remembered through the name of the housing at the end of Bremilham Road. Originally it was intended that both girls and boys would be taught here but another site was found in Cross Hayes for the girls. When this school opened on 2nd February 1857 it was proclaimed:

The object has been to provide what has long been wanted, a place of education in this town, upon such a footing that no one need be excluded on account of a religious difference; and that all classes, without distinction, may here find sound instruction, suitable to fit their children for their own sphere of employment, trade or business. Therefore, not only Reading, Writing, Arithmetic, and Needlework for girls will be taught, but Farmers and Tradesmen, who can afford to keep their children at school to an age when their minds become capable of application to higher studies, such as Geography, Mathematics and History, may provide for them a competent course of Education in this school at a moderate expense.
Mr. Henry Onesimus Moyse and Miss Facey will be the Master and Mistress of the respective schools.

The pupils of the Boys' School soon after it was taken over by Wiltshire County Council at the start of the 20th Century.

The rate of payment will be as follows:
For children whose parents are poor, 2 shillings per quarter, if paid in advance, or, if paid weekly, 2 pence halfpenny per week.
For children of Farmers, Tradesmen and others in a position superior to that of a day labourer, ten shillings per quarter, paid in advance.

Within a few years there were about 100 pupils at this school. An important part of the syllabus was gardening and land nearby was used for this purpose. The Infants had their school on the first floor until 1922 when they moved to Cross Hayes. This area became unsafe before World War II (is that why the Infants moved?) and it was only used for light storage. However with the influx of evacuees in 1940 more space was desperately needed and classes were once again held there, but the strengthening work was carried out a year later! It was not until the new Secondary Modern School opened in 1954 that this became a Primary School. In 1964 when the Grammar School vacated the site on Tetbury Hill, this school was combined with the Girls' School and moved into the old Grammar School building. The old Boys' School became the Arts Centre for the Corn Gastons School but fell into disuse in 2001.

Continue down the hill to the junction and to the right can be seen:

12 Foxley Road

This was the Plough Inn that was built around 1840. Known as the 'last and the first' for

Commoners going to work on their allotments on King's Heath, it sold only beer. It was closed in 1970 and is now a private house. In the 1950s you could have come across Harold Macmillan (1894-1986) who used to drop in for a pint of beer here during his term as Prime Minister, when he visited his daughter then living at Thornhill Farm.

The Plough Inn in 1964. It still had a Stroud Brewery Ales sign. Next to the door is a pottery West Country Ales sign. The Stroud became part of this concern in 1959 but it was swallowed up by the Whitbread empire in 1967. Although this sign, like the whitewash, has gone, other examples can still be seen on the Borough Arms, Kings Arms, Three Cups and the old White Lion.

Continue along Bristol Street up the incline.

Foxley Road to the Maltings

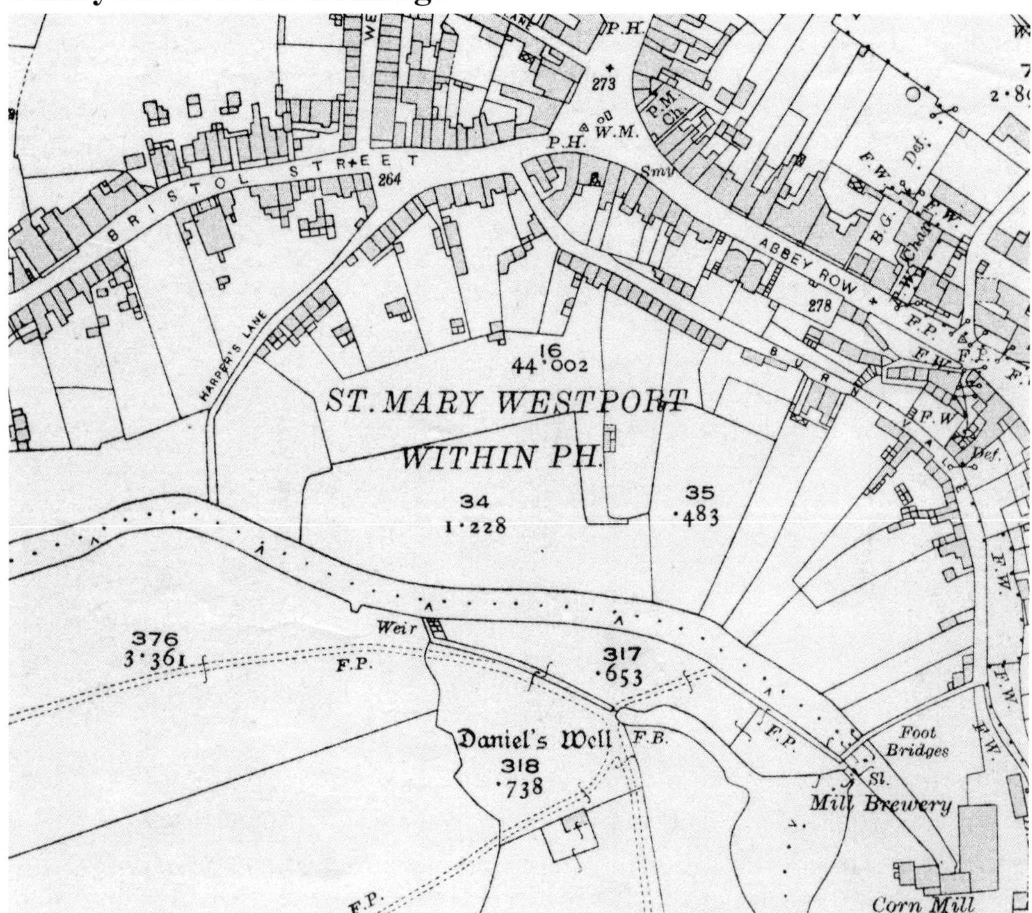

The outline of this area is largely unchanged. Notable differences can be seen bordering Betty Geezers Steps between Burnivale and Abbey Row where a number of cottages have been removed. Two modern houses have been built on the large open plot along Bristol Street.

At the top of Keene's Hill, so called because a hat maker and glover of that name had a house on the left two centuries ago, the road curves to the right where slightly set back on the right is:

Primitive Methodist Chapel, Bristol Street

The Primitives broke away from the main Methodist movement in 1812. In 1825 a group from Sherston received rough treatment from locals who regarded them as 'ranters' who had no right to be treated with civility. They withdrew after a short time. In 1854 the Brinkworth circuit, then a major centre of evangelism sending missions all over Southern England and Wales, sought to 'Mission Malmesbury'. They sang hymns and preached in the open air in Burnivale. An overzealous Church of England curate, believing they had no right to preach other than in his Church, harangued the wicked congregation and

The Bristol Street Primitive Methodist Chapel when it was used as a warehouse in the 1960s.

sought to have them banned, without success. One of the missionaries, Rev. S. Turner, described Malmesbury as *a dark, dead place*. The Primitives also used the open spaces of Horsefair and Cow Fair (Cross Hayes). The first building they used was a barn in St Mary's Lane. The foundation stone of the Bristol Street chapel was laid on 18th April 1856. Once established, the church flourished and, by 1859 was the basis of the Malmesbury Circuit. The congregation outgrew this small site and a new chapel was built in the Triangle in 1899. The old 'commodious building' was bought by Henry Poole and Frederick Poole [Burnham House], Myriorama Proprietors, for use as a studio and storerooms.

In 1905 Henry guaranteed a loan that Fred had taken out with the Wilts & Dorset Bank of up to £500. Fred died on 17 January 1907 and Henry had to pay £447 12s 7d, as the estate was otherwise insolvent. The Myriorama shows were coming to an end with the development of cinemas and so in 1909 James A. Jones, Ironmonger & Cycle Agent, bought the premises to be used as a motor garage & workshop. He ran a fleet of hire cars and this was probably their base. At the end of World War I Edwin Stuart Travis Cole took over the building. From 1932 to 1968 it was a warehouse for Coopers of Bristol, suppliers of ladies underwear and corsetry. Max Woosnam, a local personality and author of a booklet on *Eilmer*, lived in the building until 1998 when it was converted into a three-storey house.

100 yards further on there is a small terrace above the road to the north, the eastern most part of which is:

St Helens, 23 Bristol Road

This house started off in the 10th or early 11th Century as a small single cell chapel. It was set high on a natural stone platform close to the north of the Saxon Kingway that came up Harpers Lane. The large original corner stones can be seen together with the mass dial to the right of the door. It was substantially rebuilt in the 17th Century into a cottage and further additions have been made in the past 50 years.

1 West Street, (Travellers Rest Inn)

Early in the 19th Century these premises were used as a pub with a malthouse in the courtyard behind. It.was closed sometime later that century. Its yard to the east was later used by the GPO as a garage and afterwards by Cross Hayes Antiques until the modern house at 19 Bristol Road was erected in 2002.

West Street

Conservation and preservation are now key watchwords, but it is pleasant to retell a story that began nearly 40 years ago. At that time the area around West Street was in decline and did not seem to fit in with the lifestyle of the mid 20th Century. Most of the property was owned by the Borough Council or the Old Corporation. In 1967 the Council obtained outline planning permission to develop the area to the west of West Street and widen the road. To be demolished were the terraced houses at the south end of the street, together with houses in Bristol Street including the cottage subsequently identified as the Saxon St Helens Chapel. Malmesbury Civic Trust appealed for renovation rather than demolition. Further planning applications were made and granted but little work was done. In June 1974 the Civic Trust and the Council for the Protection of Rural England achieved listing of 6-30 West Street and 30-38 (even numbers) Horsefair to protect them. Notwithstanding this, the new North Wiltshire District Council ap-

The western side of West Street viewed from Bristol Street in 1964.

plied for demolition of 2-30 West Street. Fortunately they experienced difficulty in financing the project and a Stroud builder came up with an alternative scheme. After further problems were encountered the southern end of the terrace was renovated and from 18 to 22 were sympathetically rebuilt.

Just before the Triangle turn to the right down:

Burnivale

Pause at the junction and you will notice to the west that the gable end of No. 6 Bristol Street is made of modern reconstructed stone. This is because the end of terrace house, No. 4 was bought by the County Council to widen the road and the original layout is illustrated on the map. Just after turning the corner the stone wall to the north moves slightly away from the road and there are what appear to be buttresses supporting it. These are in fact the last remains of Nos, 2, 4 & 6 again demolished for road widening. As you walk along Burnivale try to work out how many of the cottages have been combined to create larger dwellings – again the Ordnance Survey will help. Burnivale acted as a bypass when tolls were in force at the town gates. From Westport it leads to the South Gate and on to the Chippenham Road.

Looking up Burnivale to the junction with Bristol Street prior to the demolition of No. 4. Articulated lorries used to come this way en route to Linolite! The sign on the wall at the left reads For Safety Turn Left at Junction.

Ragged School

Following the establishment of St. Joseph's free Roman Catholic School in 1867 [St. Aldhelm's Church], the nonconformists reacted violently and set up a committee to have it closed down. They failed to do so and instead sought to open their own school. Subscriptions were raised and the support of Walter Powell MP enlisted. He provided a wooden building put up on land donated by Charles Luce. The Ragged School, which had operated on Sundays and evenings since 1866, opened as a free day school in Burnivale (where there is now a block of garages) in February 1870 with 53 pupils, 13 of whom had come from the Catholic school. Despite a rule that no child eligible to attend the National School could be admitted, some were. The Ragged School flourished for a time with a new building being opened in June 1873. It was soon in financial difficulties but obtained its first Government grant in 1877. However as more funding came from the State, so the cost of meeting their standards rose. The financial difficulties were so great that parents were charged 1½d. per week. Apparently if not all of this could be afforded then the pupil attended for part of the week. By 1886 it was too expensive to comply with current requirements and the school closed with the pupils transferring to the National Schools.

The narrowness of Burnivale illustrated near the foot of Betty Geezers Steps. The buildings on the left have been demolished but their site is marked by different stone in the wall.

At the end of the road you enter a housing development called:

The Maltings

This is one of the few sites in the old town where an archaeological investigation has been carried out. During the Roman period there was a brick kiln here and Roman coins have been found. The Saxons also had a kiln and tiles similar to those discovered under the Abbey floor were found here. There was a tannery & slaughterhouse for 400 years during medieval times with many animal bones in evidence. Later there was a corn mill, followed in the 16th Century by a woollen mill owned by Matthew Kyng MP. He lived where Kings House is and it is thought that the name Kings Wall is associated with him. With the decline of the woollen industry it reverted to the milling of grain. In 1836 the site was bought by Thomas Luce [35 High Street] and developed into a brewery and malt house.

Thomas, the Bank Manager, had started brewing in 1821 when he entered into a partnership with John Brooke. They bought the brewery in the Cross Hayes for £2,200, with only £200 put up by Brooke who managed the business. When Luce sold the bank in 1836 he reinvested the proceeds in new premises. His son Charles (1829-1926) took over the brewery and as the Bank Manager from his father in 1851, about the time that Thomas was elected to Parliament. Because his main concern was the bank he took a partner, Mr. Harris, who oversaw the brewery. This relationship broke down 12 years later when a private auction was held between the partners in the Kings Arms. Eventually with the support of his brother-in-law, Charles made the highest bid. He then hired a manager, Mr. Farrow who remained with the business for nearly 50 years. In 1865 a serious fire necessitated much rebuilding. A new malthouse was erected in 1887.

Charles groomed his eldest son Edward (1863-1887) to take over the business, however he died from typhoid [Whole Hog]. Then his youngest son Cecil (1873-1901) was intended to take his place. He was an enthusiastic Volunteer officer and joined the Wiltshire Regiment for the Boer War. Unfortunately in South Africa he too succumbed to typhoid. So with no one to succeed him Charles sold the business to the Stroud Brewery Company in 1912. The main reason for the Stroud's purchase was the 42 licensed premises owned by Luce including 13 in Malmesbury. Licensees often had little money and bought beer on credit from Brewers. To safeguard their position the supplies would be secured on the main asset – the pub building. If the publican was unable to pay, the

The Malthouse just before demolition in the mid 1980s. Many thought that this striking building could have been retained.

brewery would foreclose on the pub. At the end of WWI after the introduction of stricter licensing laws, the Stroud had to rationalise their production and they closed many small breweries including Luce's.

In 1923 Edwards and Armstrong Company, owners of the Malmesbury Electricity Supply Company, with the backing of Captain Scott Mackirdy [Abbey House] bought the Brewery to produce electricity. A Special Order entitled 'Malmesbury Electricity' was issued by the Minister in August of that year. It gave the Western Electric Distributing Corporation Ltd. permission to supply mains electricity within a 1 mile radius of the North-west corner of the Abbey building, particularly in Gloucester Street from Bristol Street to Market Cross, High Street, Oxford Street from Market Cross to the Town Hall, Cross Hayes Lane and Cross Hayes. Part of the Postern Mill brew house was used to make gas to operate two large gas engines which drove generators. Advantage was taken of the water power by installing a water turbine. Unfortunately even then the flow was often insufficient and there was a WWI tank engine in reserve. The bottling hall housed a huge bank of glass sided batteries as the power was Direct Current. In 1929 the Company was bought by the Western Electricity Supply Co. Ltd. which later became Wessex Electricity. When the grid was extended to the town in the early 1930s Alternating Current was introduced and all of the plant became redundant. The buildings were then just used for storage.

In 1941 Linolite Ltd. moved into the old mill. Alfred Beutell had patented a tubular electric lamp in 1901. After making some himself he contracted Edison and Swan to make them. He formed his own company that took over production and was renamed Linolite Ltd. in 1933. They made filament strip lights, often used for displays and later for shaving lamps. During the Second World War they concentrated on being the main supplier of hose clips for bomber aircraft de-icing systems. Unfortunately their factory was in Victoria - they were finally told by the Ministry of Aircraft Production to evacuate from London and they chose Malmesbury. A lease was granted by Wessex Electricity. During the war Linolite made 7.5 million hose clips in a workshop on the third floor of the mill. The second floor was their canteen with offices on the first. In 1944 there was a disastrous fire that badly damaged the upper part of the building and the adjacent Electricity Manager's dwelling. The building was covered with a new asbestos roof but the top 2 floors were never reused. The malting which had been unused since the closure of the brewery became a National Reserve Food Store. After the war Linolite reverted to making electric lights and new buildings were erected. The brewery was unoccupied and deteriorated over the years. In 1985 the company moved to new premises at the top of Tetbury Hill. Finally the factory, then part of the Concord Rotaflex Group, closed in 1993 putting nearly 200 people out of work. Later the factory was taken over by Dyson. The Maltings housing project, originally proposed for older people, was finally built in 1989 after the first contractor went out of business.

Postern Gate to High Street

The Maltings replace not only the Mill and Malthouse but also most of the orchard to the south. The upper part of the millstream has been filled in but the southern half of the island remains as open ground. A few new houses have been built along Kings Wall.

Walk up the slope to your left and you pass the site of the Postern Gate up the steps on the left. Continue beyond where the footway narrows into Kings Wall. As you walk down the slope on the left is a narrow footpath between high stone walls – King's Walk. This was provided by J.E. Ponting [43a High Street] when he built the Post Office. He wanted to use the name 'King Edward the Seventh's Walk' but the Borough Council asked for it to be abbreviated. Also known as the Twopenny Tube, it is reminiscent of the 'cut and cover' underground railways that were being built in London at the beginning of the 20th Century, the fare for which was 2d. A few yards further on is a road to the right which leads to:

St. Aldhelm's Mead

This was supposed to have been given to the Abbey by Queen Mathilda, wife of William the Conqueror, as the site for a fair to be held on St. Aldhelms's feast day, 25th May. In Norman times this extended over a number of days varying from three to eight. With the passage of time the area became privately owned. However in 1933 the Luce family presented it to the town for use as a recreation ground in memory of Charles Luce, the first Mayor and his son, Admiral John Luce, who had died the previous year. In 1948 a children's play area was constructed.

If you have resisted the temptation for a walk in the park, at the end of the terrace on the right stands:

Kings House

The East End was built around 1700 and the house was extended west and north soon afterwards with old-fashioned mullion and transomed windows. There are two possible explanations for the name. First, it is reputed to have been the site of King Athelstan's palace, but I discount this as it is outside the town's defences. More likely it was where Matthew Kyng, MP and clothier lived in the 16th Century. He was an unscrupulous character who always seemed to be on the wrong side of the law, frequently appearing in the civil and criminal courts although he represented the town in Parliament between

Kings House. The two armorial crests can be seen on the parapet. The high boundary wall obscures this view.

1554 and 1558. Early in the 19th Century Benjamin Coffin Thomas (1776-1840) owned the house and he invited William Cobbett (1763-1835) to stay here. Cobbett wrote the following account in *Rural Rides* on 11 September 1826 which is so engaging I reproduce it in full:

When I got in here yesterday, I went, at first, to an inn; but I very soon changed my quarters for the house of a friend, who and whose family, though I had never seen them before, and had never heard of them until I was at Highworth, gave me a hearty reception, and precisely in the style that I like. This town, though it has nothing particularly engaging in itself, stands upon one of the prettiest spots that can be imagined. Besides the river Avon, which I went down in the south-east part of the country, here is another river Avon, which runs down to Bath, and two branches, or sources, of which meet here. There is a pretty ridge of ground, the base of which is a mile or a mile and a half wide. On each side of this ridge a branch of the river runs down, through a flat of very fine meadows. The town and the beautiful remains of the famous old abbey stand on the rounded spot which terminates this ridge; and, just below, nearly close to the town, the two branches of the river meet; and then they begin to be called the Avon. The land round about is excellent, and of a great variety of forms. The trees are lofty and fine: so that what with the water, the meadows, the fine cattle and sheep, and, as I hear, the absence of hard-pinching poverty, this is a very pleasant place. There remains more of the abbey than, I believe, of any of our monastic buildings, except that of Westminster, and those that have become cathedrals. The church service is performed in the part of the abbey that is left standing. The parish church has fallen down and is gone; but the tower remains, which is made use of for the bells; but the abbey is used as the church, though the church-tower is at a considerable distance from it. It was once a most magnificent building; and there is now a doorway which is the most beautiful thing I ever saw, and which was, nevertheless, built in Saxon times, in "the dark ages," and was built by men who were not begotten by Pitt nor by Jubilee George. – What fools, as well as ungrateful creatures we have been and are! There is a broken arch, standing off from the sound part of the building, at which one cannot look up without feeling shame at the thought of ever having abused the men who made it. No one need tell any man of sense; he feels our inferiority to our fathers upon merely beholding the remains of their efforts to ornament their country and elevate the minds of the people. We talk of our skill and learning, indeed! How do we know how skilful, how learned they were? If, in all that they have left us, we see they have surpassed us, why are we to conclude that they did not surpass us in all other things worthy of admiration?

This famous abbey was founded, in about the year 600, by Maidulf, a Scotch monk, who upon the suppression of a nunnery at that time selected the spot for this great establishment. For the great magnificence, however, to which it was soon after brought, it was indebted to Aldhelm, a monk educated within its first walls, by the founder himself; and to St. Aldhelm, who by his great virtues became very famous, the church was dedicated in the time of King Edgar. This monastery continued flourishing during those dark ages, until it was found to be endowed to the amount of sixteen thousand and seventy seven

pounds, eleven shillings and eight pence. of the money of the present day! Amongst other, many other, great men produced by this Abbey of Malmsbury, was that famous scholar and historian, William de Malmsbury.
There is a market-cross in this town, the sight of which is worth a journey of hundreds of miles. Time, with his scythe, and 'enlightened Protestant piety,' with its pick-axes and crow-bars; these united have done much to efface the beauties of this monument of ancient skill and taste, and proof of ancient wealth; but in spite of all their destructive efforts this cross still remains a most beautiful thing, though possibly, and even probably, nearly, or quite, a thousand years old. There is a market-cross lately erected at Devizes, and intended to imitate the ancient ones. Compare that with this, and you have, pretty fair, a view of the difference between us and our fore-fathers of the 'dark ages.'
I set off from Malmsbury this morning at 6 o'clock, in as sweet and bright a morning as ever came out of the heavens, and leaving behind me as pleasant a house and as kind hosts as I ever met with in the whole course of my life, either in England or America, and that is saying a great deal indeed. This circumstance was the more pleasant, as I had never before seen, or heard of, these kind, unaffected, sensible, sans-façons, and most agreeable friends.

Cobbett was a Radical who had scathing words for any small example of corruption and mismanagement that he found on his tours. The hospitality he received must have been excellent for him not to mention anything about this rotten borough or that his host was one of the chief aides of the borough-monger. Thomas was Clerk to the Magistrates, to the Lieutenancy and to the Commissioner of Taxes and carried on that business here so that may be the reason for the Old Corporation's arms on the roofline nearest the river. The crest closest to the road is probably that of the Anderson and Yeaman families but it is not known what their connection was with the house. The house was later divided into two or three separate dwellings.

High Street to Burton Hill

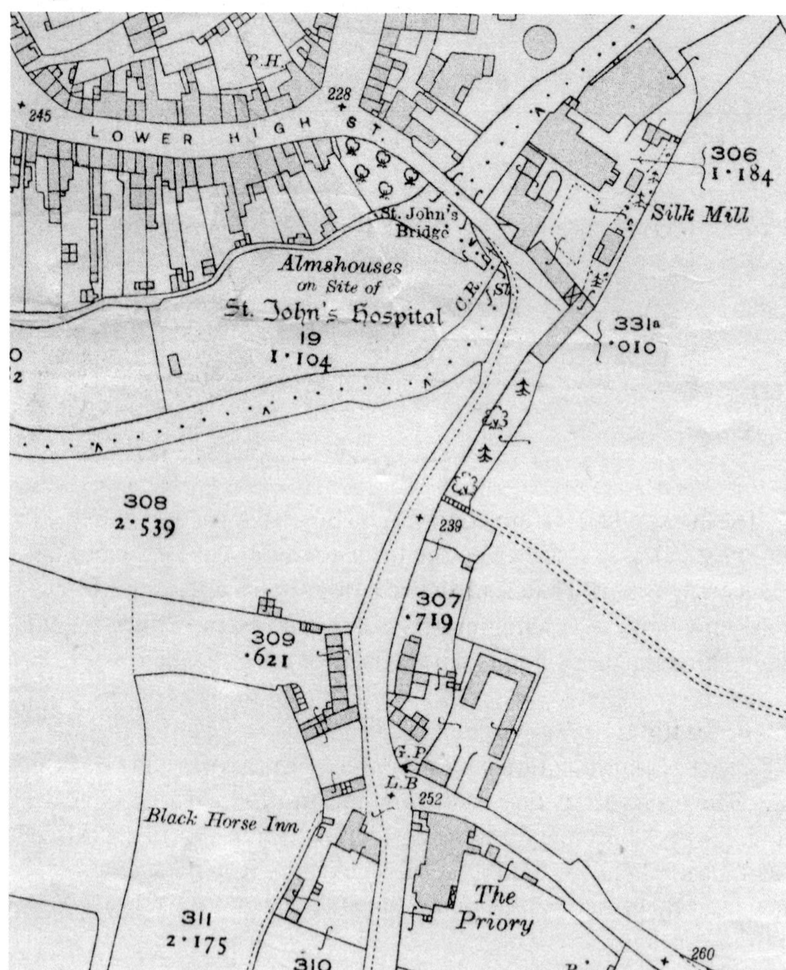

The large building behind the Silk Mill has been demolished and replaced with a terrace of houses.There is no trace left of the Black Horse Inn, the Priory or the farm to the north of it, although the road junction is still to the west of the roundabout. The 'four and twenty steps' field used by the Boxing Club in the 1950s is between the Silk Mill and Priory Farm. Barley Close and Orchard Court were built in the 1970s in the field marked 311 behind the Inn.

Continue along Kings Wall to the junction with the Lower High Street. Pause to look at the curious curved wall of the cottage on the left believed to be part of the South Gate bastion. The position of the gate is shown in the footpath and there is a descriptive bronze plaque across the road. Continue until just before the bridge on the right hand side is:

Second World War Memorial

Before the Second World War ended the Borough Council began discussing what form the war memorial should take. There was a heated debate over whether an improvement to the hospital or a recreation ground was most appropriate. In the end the memorial gates and small garden at the entrance to St Aldhelm Mead were chosen. The owner of the Silk Mill, H.G. Kattan gave the land and the Women's Institute collected £300 of the £565 8s. cost of the pillars and gates. The bronze plaques amounted to a further £91 5s.

The blessing of the new Second World War memorial gates. Wreaths are still laid here every Remembrance Sunday.

4d. plus £40 for fitting. Twenty servicemen are commemorated on the gateposts. One of these is Flight Sergeant Bernard Basevi, known before the war for his Carnival entertainments, particularly for his escapes from chains and a sack under water next to the Town Bridge. His plane ditched on his first bombing mission and he died at sea from exposure. Lord Haw-Haw mentioned his fate in one of his radio broadcasts.

St John's (or the Town) Bridge

There has been a bridge here for many centuries. In the 1648 bird's eye map it is shown as a wooden drawbridge. The present structure dates from the mid 19th Century. Note on the eastern parapet in the centre a short metal stanchion. This is the remains of a gas lamp that used to light the road. When James Jones [H.J. Knee Ltd.] was Mayor, he had this removed as he could not see why the Borough Council should pay to light the Rural District Council's half of the bridge!

Across the bridge the large buildings are:

Avon Mill

This is one of the sites around the town where there was a mill back into the mists of antiquity. Schotesbure Mill stood here in the 13th Century. By the middle of the 16th Century the millers came from the Cannop family and the mill took their name. Nicholas Archard, whose family had owned the Burton Hill estate during this time, built a new fulling mill here around 1600. Fulling was the process whereby cloth was thickened and shrunk by pounding it in a solution of fullers earth. The outbreak of the 30 Years' War in 1620 had cut off export markets, causing a crisis in the woollen industry leading to the spectacular failure of Archard's business in 1622. However these premises were still known as Archard's Mill when the bird's-eye map was prepared in 1648. The first building across the bridge is the Mill House which dates from 1720.

The woollen industry in Malmesbury was cyclical and a century later it had closed down. At that time machinery was being introduced to the industry in the face of fierce opposition of the workers. Francis Hill, a Bradford on Avon clothier and lawyer bought this mill in 1790 to reintroduce the trade to the town. He moved his business from Bradford following riots there when he proposed to use new machines, a matter described to a Parliamentary commission in 1803. He built the two factory buildings in 1793 only 20 years after the first ever factory had been built by Richard Arkwright in Derbyshire. Factories organised labour in one specialised workplace giving the employer total control over the means and cost of production. Hill pioneered the use in Wiltshire of water power to drive fly shuttles and some 50 or 60 spring looms for weaving. Although vast quantities of cloth could be produced the quality was poor and much of the product was returned to the factory. It was fortunate that he was able to supply cloth to the government for uniforms during the Napoleonic Wars. Although Hill's business was innovative it was unsuccessful and closed before his death in 1828.

C.S. Taylor & Co. of Chippenham then rented the factory for a short period. They introduced spinning mules but went bankrupt in 1830. In 1831 when the town was surveyed by Benjamin Ansley for the Great Reform Bill he noted; *a cloth factory was established about 20 years ago; but is now abandoned, and has been converted into a corn-mill. It (the town) contains very few Houses which appear to be occupied by persons of independent circumstances, and has altogether the air of a place on the decline, it must now be considered as entirely an agricultural Town.* Maybe there is a lesson for the present here about dependence on one large employer. After a wrangle over Francis Hill's will, the mill as part of the estate was bought by Simon Uncles Salter (1800-1851) and his brother Isaac in 1833. Five years later a steam engine was in use.

The Silk Mill about 1900. The footpath and footbridge were not made until the 1960s.

This was unusual as a lot of coal was needed to power the engine. There was no canal which was the normal way of carrying heavy bulky goods and the road network to the town was none too good. Around 1840 a Highland regiment camped on the Worthies and proved such an attraction to the young women who worked in the factory that it had to shut until the soldiers moved on!

Thomas Bridget & Co. of Derby bought the mill in 1852. They were silk manufacturers but sold the factory 15 years later. Richard Jefferies described the operation in 1867; *the silk arrives here in a raw state and is unpacked in the upper storeys of the building. Much of it is Chinese, and the packages often contain small slips of paper stamped with Chinese characters. The operation of cleaning employs a large number of children who tend the machinery used for that purpose. Most of these are very young and sing at their work. Overseers superintend them, and talking is not allowed, for the simple reason that attention is required to be exercised to manipulate the silk properly. Beneath is the winding department; lower still the looms where the ribbons are made. The machinery is of an order impossible to describe. There is a sameness in it. Apparently the greatest attention is paid to the comfort of those employed. The rooms are very large, well lighted, and though necessarily warm, not overheated. Nevertheless, from being so early put to work the children have an old look; but nothing of that careworn expression sometimes seen in factories. The machinery is driven by water power.* Silk ribbons were much in demand during the Victorian era and at its peak the factory employed around 400. A tariff on silk products was removed in 1860 and it was difficult to compete with imports, particularly from France. Unfortunately the business failed in 1889, but before the end of the century was reopened by Jupe's of Mere and by 1900 there were 150 workers. Japanese competition forced another closure that year but in the early 1920s production was restored by Avon Silk Mills Co. Ltd. Residents of the town could tell the time by the Silk Mill's bell which first sounded at five o'clock in the morning, then for breakfast at eight o'clock, lunch at one o'clock and finally at six in the evening. Silk production continued until 1941 when the Ministry of Supply closed it down. Most of the 200 workers were transferred to Ekco [Cowbridge House]. Dryden & Son bought the premises in 1950 to be used for dressing rabbit skins. Unfortunately myxomatosis, which was introduced to control the rabbit population, instead decimated it and brought that business to an end in 1954. The owners then opened an antiques showroom that carried on until 1980. Other businesses operated from the site, between 1974 and 1979 Manco produced battery chargers but made 30 workers redundant when they closed. In 1984 both buildings were converted to flats.

The area to the right of the right of the walkway leading to the footbridge was originally called 'Cucking Stool Mead', so called because it was where errant women were 'corrected' by ducking them in the river. Whilst Avon Mill produced cloth it was stretched here on racks to dry after fulling thus becoming 'Rack Meadow'. 'Black Meadow' was behind the factory where dyestuff was thrown from the windows! There was also a grand celebration here to celebrate the passing of the Great Reform Act. Tuesday 21 August 1832 was the date chosen but many hours of rain caused it to be postponed after 13 extensive tables had been erected and four hogsheads of beer delivered. Bird [King's Nursery] described it thus: *The morning of Wednesday opened with every appearance of the weather clearing up. The bands of music played throughout the streets, whilst crowds of people in their holiday attire were pouring in from the adjacent parts, presenting a scene of the most animating description. The principal shops being closed, at 2 o'clock a procession of professional gentlemen and tradesmen paraded the different streets of the town arm-in arm, preceeded by bands of music, and thirty handsome flags and banners. On the approach of the Procession to the entrance of the field the number of persons congregated was so dense as to render it almost impossible to stir. The gates, at which Officers were stationed, being opened, those who possessed tickets, amounting to nearly 2,000, were admitted to the tables. At a cross table at either extremity of the field was a baron of roast beef of enormous dimensions, each surmounted by a small dark-blue flag, bearing the inscription, "The Roast Beef of Old England." Just previous to the sitting down to dinner, at the sound of the bugle, the Band struck up the tune "God save the King" which the assembled multitude joined in singing the following lines written for the occasion as a Grace - no Clergyman being present to engage in so important a duty.*

TUNE,—" God save the King."
Author of ev'ry good,
Bless to our use this food
What Thou dost give;
Grant we may always see,
That blessings flow from Thee,
Now, let us thankful be,
And while we live.

At the conclusion of the dinner, which was of the most inviting nature, and during the evening, the usual loyal and patriotic toasts were given and heartily responded to. The aggregate quantity of viands amounted to 2 oxen, 4 sheep, about 600 half-quartern loaves, and upwards of 80 plum-puddings, besides 8 hogs-heads of strong beer. On the following day the remains were distributed to nearly 100 poor families.
Such an assemblage was never before witnessed in the town; it being computed that there were at one time not less than four thousand persons in the field; every commanding position outside the gates being thronged. The evening concluded with a grand display of Fireworks.

And I expect that the town will never see anything similar again!

Continue over the bridge and past the water meadow there is a terrace alongside the road on the right. This is Parliament Row built because one of the Salter brothers [Burton Hill House] wished to stand for parliament and thought he could create some sympathetic voters by building them houses, but he was not elected. Just beyond this is the original junction where the Chippenham and Swindon roads met before the bypass was built in 1973.

Burton Hill

South of the roundabout, BT built their digital exchange in the 1970s which is probably redundant now. Next to this are the 1950s Police houses and Station. The Station may move in the near future. The access to the small housing estate of Orchard Court is off Arches Lane. At the end of the lane Arches Farm is no longer a working farm. A number of extensions have been added to both the Manor House and Burton Hill House, to cater for their modern uses.

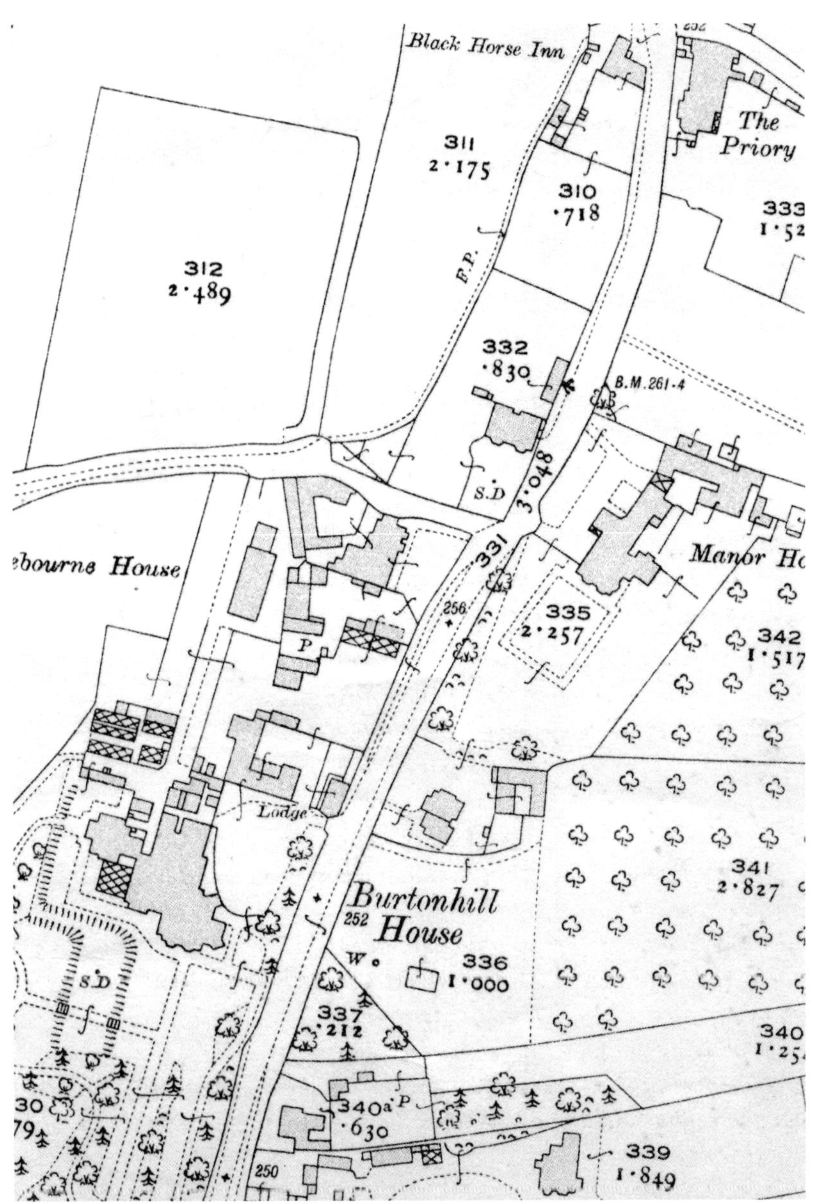

To the right the Black Horse Inn stood between the 19th Century and 1971 and on the left was:

The Priory

Unfortunately nothing now remains of this house. It was to the east of the approach to the roundabout. In the 13th Century the hospital of St Mary Magdalene stood here. The chapel survived and was later used as a private house. In the early 18th Century this was demolished and a new house, Canister Hall, was built on the site. In 1809 Richard Robins [Lloyds TSB] bought the house and obviously finding it unfashionable and not suitable for his status, built a new three-storey brick house and changed the name to the Priory. His widow, Hester Robins sold the house to Simon Salter [Burton Hill House] in 1842 until 1865 when Thomas Henry Chubb (1815-1888) bought it. He was a solicitor whose father Thomas [Stainsbridge House] set up a practice which became Chubb & Sons with an office at 36 Cross Hayes. His sons Montagu Henry (1855-1942) and Alfred William were trustees under their father's will. Montague Chubb carried out many public functions having been appointed Town Clerk and Clerk to the Magistrates in 1874. He became first Clerk to the Joint Burial Board in 1882, first Clerk to the 'new' Corporation in 1886, Deputy High Steward 1888 and High Steward in 1918, as well as being Clerk to the Rural District Council and holding many other posts in surrounding villages. He was given the Freedom of the Borough in 1935 on his 80th birthday, after 50 years service to the Borough Council. At the beginning of the 20th Century Lewis Edward Morrice (1853-1933) bought the house. He had served with the Royal Warwickshire Regiment in the Boer War where he awarded the Distinguished Service Order. After his death his widow lived here until she died. During the last war workers at Ekco used the house and it was converted into flats. In 1967 a fire caused substantial damage which was not repaired and the remains were demolished to make way for the bypass. Priory Farm, to the north of the Swindon Road, was also owned by this household before the Second World War. The

The Chippenham Road with the Priory on the right and the Black Horse Inn in the distance on the left.

farmer at that time, Bill Woodward, is remembered for sitting in the dairy ladling out creamy milk to children who came to collect it.

Continuing south just before the junction of Arches Lane is:

The Beeches, Burton Hill

This house was built in the late 18th Century. Two hundred years later it was a residential home for the elderly for over 20 years until 1999 and is now a private house again. Esau Duck [32 Cross Hayes] and his family lived here from the early 1880s until his widow's death in 1910. It was then rented to Mrs Ramsay, niece of the Dowager Countess of Suffolk who lived here until World War II, for the grand sum of £45 per annum. Later Alfred Beutell [Postern Mill] occupied the house when he was running Linolite during and after that war.

Burton Hill School

50 metres past Arches Lane there is the wall surrounding this house with its entrance. The original house here was probably built in the early 17th Century. In 1787 Timothy Dewall [32 Cross Hayes], a doctor who practised in Malmesbury bought it for £2,650. Following his death the property was auctioned on 3rd November 1792 when Francis Hill, a lawyer and clothier from Bradford-upon-Avon paid £3,610. He had bought the mill by the Town Bridge two years before and was rebuilding that. Five years after his death in 1828, Simon and Isaac Salter of Kington Langley purchased the house together with Burton Hill Mill (later to become the Silk Mill) for £7,500. The Salters sold Burton Hill House with 35 acres to John Cockerell from London in 1842 for £7,050. Cockerell pulled the house down and employed his brother Charles Robert Cockerell (1788-1863) to design a new house. Charles was the most gifted and knowledgeable architect of his day. At the same time as he was supervising the construction of his brother's home, he was completing one of his finest commissions, the Ashmolean Museum in Oxford. Unfortunately Burton Hill House burnt down on 14th March 1846 when the damage was estimated at £10,000. Rebuilding started immediately using the same Tudor-Gothic design but three years later Charles William Miles (who was known as Peter!) bought the house.

Miles was a member of an old family of bankers and merchants from Bristol, had been a Lieutenant Colonel commanding the 17th Lancers and hunted with the Quorn before coming to Malmesbury. He became High Sheriff of Wiltshire and High Steward in 1856. He wanted the house to be known as Ingleburn (also spelt Ingleburne or Inglebourne) Manor. He made many changes to the structure notably an extension to the west including a ballroom. G. G. Scott Junior was the architect who oversaw the works and some of his moulded plaster ceilings survive. After Peter Miles died in 1892 the house passed to his son Charles Napier Miles (1854-1918). He was also an army officer who had been commissioned into the Life Guards in 1875. Charles served in Egypt during 1882 and in the South African War, being mentioned in dispatches. He commanded 1st Life Guards

Burton Hill House at the beginning of the 20th Century. Much work was done in the gardens during the 1920s and 30s.

from 1895 to 1902 and became a CB and MVO. He became involved in local affairs being a magistrate and the High Steward of the Old Corporation from 1893 until his death. His wife Emelye converted to Catholicism, and this is commemorated by a crucifix in St Aldhelms Church dated 1903. They had no children and Napier's brother Audley Charles Miles inherited but he died in 1919. Later that year parts of the estate amounting to 200 acres were sold off at auction in the Kings Arms, presumably because of death duties. The owner was Thomas Gordon Audley Miles who advertised the house and the remaining 174 acres in Country Life during 1921.

However it was not until 1924 that H L Storey [Hospital] bought the estate. He moved from Burton Hill Manor, which he sold for use as the hospital. Again more improvements were made including the construction of a large lake in the grounds, apparently work instigated to provide employment during the depression. He died in 1933. His widow moved across the road to East Cottage and sought to sell the house. Finding no buyer, it was leased to Misses 'Zoo' and Hilary Hunt around 1936, who set up a private school. Nursery education was provided for local children, both day and boarding. This establishment closed in 1945. By this time the estate incorporated over 150 acres which was sold in lots. Shortly afterwards Mrs. Storey was finally able to sell the house, which included Arches Farm, to the Shaftesbury Society for £11,000. Their school for up to 50 handicapped girls opened on 1st May 1947. Boys joined the roll in 1961. In 1964 a hydrotherapy pool costing £10,500 was built.

Crossing the road and walking back towards the roundabout there is:

Malmesbury Community Hospital

Originally this was a farmhouse that by 1823 was called the Manor House. It was rebuilt later in the 19th Century in Tudor style, probably by Col Peter Miles who incorporated it into the Burton Hill Estate. Colonel Charles Miles allowed the Red Cross to use the Manor House as a hospital for the duration of the First World War. In 1919 it was bought by Herbert Lushington Storey, the eldest son of Sir Thomas Storey (1825-1898). In the middle of the 19th Century William Storey (1823-1879), Herbert's uncle, started a painting, japanning and tablecover manufacturing business in Lancaster. William was joined by his younger brother Thomas and the business rapidly expanded. In 1887 Sir Thomas purchased the Bailrigg estate comprising 784 acres, four farms and other properties. In 1898, the year of his father's death, Herbert began to build a 12 bedroomed mansion which took the same name as the estate. The house and garden were designed by Thomas Hayton Mawson a noted Lancastrian architect. Herbert was a keen horseman and hunter and wanted to join the Beaufort Hunt. Therefore he bought the Manor House and spent part of the year here. After a couple of years he decided to dispose of Bailrigg which was sold at auction on 1st November 1921. Within a short time he found that there was not enough room for his expanding stable and in 1924 he moved across the road into Burton Hill House.

Joe Moore [Old Bell Hotel], the Chairman of the Managers of the Malmesbury Cottage Hospital who wished to move the Hospital from the Market Cross, bought it at auction in London on 29th July 1925 for £8,000 from H.L. Storey. The house had seven bedrooms,

A photograph from the sales particulars for Burton Hill Manor House in 1925.

The front of the hospital had not changed much by 1964.

two bathrooms, a bath dressing room, five servants' bedrooms with one bathroom, five reception rooms and 'Domestic Offices' comprising a lofty kitchen, scullery, butler's pantry, brushing room and servants' hall. The old hospital was closed on 12th December 1925 and was subsequently sold for £4,870. The Countess of Suffolk agreed to sell the Maternity wing (which used what is now Abbeyfield House) for £1,000 and this sum was donated to the project. The new premises were opened on 16th January 1926, having cost a further £2,414 15s. 4d. to adapt. Here there was an operating theatre, 30 beds, five private wards and six maternity beds, as well as accommodation for staff and an on-site laundry. The staff comprised a matron, two sisters, two staff nurses, five probationers and a sister midwife. At this time there was a weekly report in the local papers recording those who had made gifts to the hospital, which usually comprised vegetables, flowers, cakes, meat or papers. Up until the National Health Service Act 1946 the Carnival continued to contribute funds to the hospital.

The services offered by the hospital expanded over the years - an Ear, Nose and Throat Clinic was added in 1930, a Heart Clinic in 1931 and a Speech Therapist after 1947. The Malmesbury Community Hospital is now run by the Kennet and North Wiltshire Primary Care Trust. The future of the hospital seems to have been under review for a considerable time and the facilities have diminished. Around 1990 the operating theatre closed but a few years later a day surgical unit for minor procedures was opened. The Maternity Unit, despite being lauded as a centre of excellence, is now considered to be uneconomic.

Until the end of the 1990s the Minor Injuries Unit offered 24-hour cover but is now only open during the day. Many outpatient clinics are held each month. The hospital now specialises in nursing of the elderly, convalescence and terminal care, as well as maternity cases for the time being. Also using the same site is a Physiotherapy Department, Occupational Therapy and an X-Ray Department. The Primary Care Trust have concluded that the building has reached the end of its useful life and intends to develop a new facility in partnership with a private contractor and the town's General Practice. This will incorporate a new surgery and care home and should be complete in 2007.

Police Station

A new station opened at Burton Hill in 1955 when that in Burnham Road was vacated. Since the Police and Magistrates Courts Act 1994, the police have been controlled by a free standing Police Authority comprised of nine local councillors, three magistrates and five appointed independent members. Prior to that the Police Authority was a committee of Wiltshire County Council. The force is financed through central government and local government grants, together with a precept on Council Tax.

Wiltshire Constabulary have used a helicopter in their Air Support Unit for several years. Since December 1998 this has been a Boeing MD 902 Explorer. This responds to about 1,100 incidents each year, carries a paramedic and often acts as an air ambulance. This aircraft is often seen in the skies above the town.

The Malmesbury station, open to the public from 10-12am but fully operative 24 hours a day, 365 days per year, now takes care of an area of over 110 square miles and has one Sergeant, ten Constables and one Police Community Support Officer (PCSO). There is also a Local Investigation Officer to assist with the gathering of evidence, three Special Constables who are often on duty at weekends and a station volunteer to help keep paperwork under control. PCSOs are a new innovation introduced in the last few years mainly to deal with anti social behaviour. Although tackling this issue it has meant the removal of traffic wardens which has led to less regulation of bad parkers! The station is part of C Division, with headquarters in Melksham which is responsible for the areas covered by both West Wiltshire and North Wiltshire District Councils.

Burton Hill to the Knoll

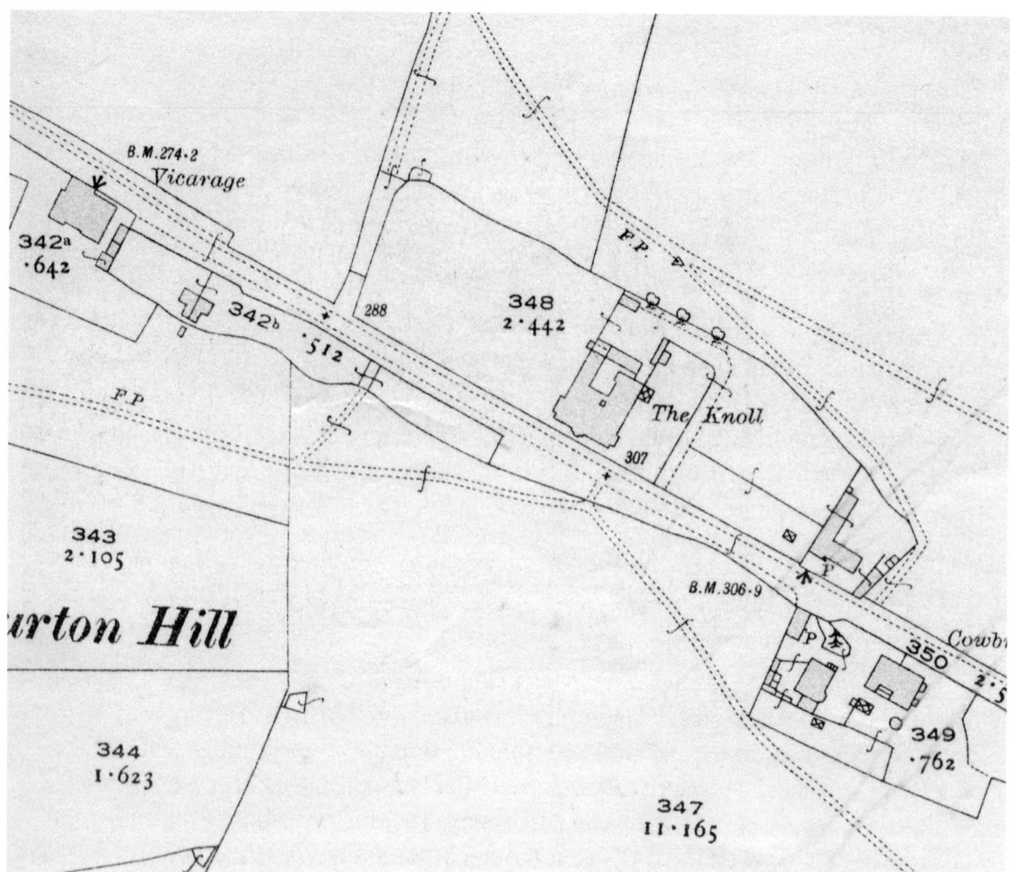

Now we take the turning on the right at the roundabout for a short excursion along the Swindon Road. A new vicarage for the St. Paul's parish was erected in 1880 on the Swindon Road just 50 yards on the right along from the roundabout. Originally the Vicarage for the parish priest was next to the White Lion in Gloucester Street. Swindon Road was less convenient for the incumbent and more recently the vicar has used a house on the corner of Holloway. Unfortunately the Swindon Road Vicarage was demolished in 2000 and four executive homes have replaced it.

Knoll House, Swindon Road
Just before the brow of the hill on the left is the Knoll. This was apparently built as the family home of Captain William Luce RN (1794-1874) brother of Thomas [Lloyds TSB], probably during the 1840s. It was also home to his son William Hollis Luce (1822-1912) who had four daughters, Gertrude (1871-1962), Jane (1872-1937), Ursula (1874-1965), Amy (1879-1967) and two sons, Thomas (1877-1925), William (1880-1900). Before World War II the sisters distributed vouchers worth 5s. to the poor of the town that were redeemable at Adye's Grocers at 52 High Street. Ursula would park her

Knoll House viewed from the south at the start of the 20th Century.

car outside the shop, toot her horn and expect David Adye to serve her at the kerbside! Gertrude was a JP and School Governor. Amy smoked Turkish cigarettes and organised local National Savings. She expected to be able to jump the queue at the Post Office where at least one assistant sought to thwart her! Each sister had her own car and even during the war would drive separately to the Abbey. There was no family member to continue to use the house after Amy's death. After 1988 the building was used as an hotel and was extended to increase the accommodation. Unfortunately after the closure of Lucent [Cowbridge House], the hotel closed. The extension was demolished, the original house turned into 3 dwellings, with other new houses built in the grounds. Unfortunately during the redevelopment work was interrupted when the body of a murdered young woman was discovered concealed on the site.

Cowbridge

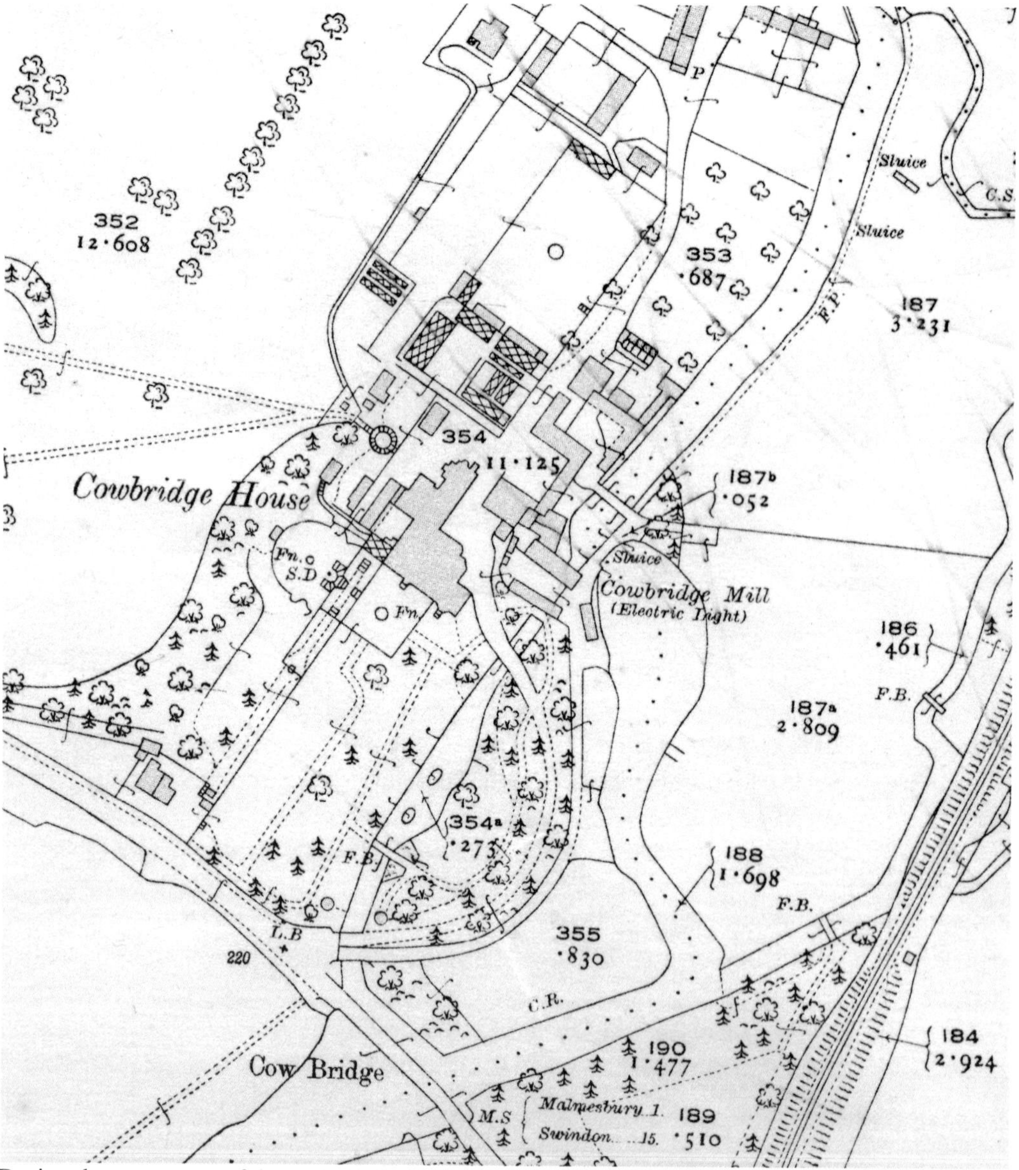

During the war, many of the outbuildings were demolished to be replaced by utilitarian structures. Just to the south west of the house, a few wooden huts were erected on the terrace. They survived in good condition into the new millenium.

Continue over the brow of the hill and part way down the slope on the left is:

Cowbridge Crescent

12 council houses and prefabs were constructed in Cowbridge Crescent between 1941

The aluminium prefabricated bungalows of Cowbridge Crescent in the mid 1960s.

and 1948 for workers at the E.K. Cole factory. Another 26 aluminium bungalows were erected for Ekco workers in 1948 which cost the Council £49,624 but a Government grant contributed £17,524 of this. During the 1970s and 80s they were replaced by normal houses and more were added.

Cowbridge House

At the bottom of the hill just before the bridge is what appears to be a modern office. By 1773 there was a large house and mill (Cow Mill) on this site. In 1839 Samuel Bendry Brooke bought the property and in 1849/50 he rebuilt the house in an Italianate/French style. When he died in 1869 his nephew, Rev. Charles Kemble, the Rector of Bath, inherited. Kemble carried out some improvements to the house (his initials can be seen on railings that used to be part of the bridge over the mill stream at the entrance), but is best known for dealing with the restoration of Bath Abbey 1864-74 using George Gilbert Scott Junior as architect. On Kemble's death his widow Charlotte then settled it on their son Stephen. He offered it for sale from 1893 and in 1899 Baldomero de Bertodano, a retired Spanish solicitor who had practised in Swindon purchased it. The mill, which previously had been used by a brewer, was used to generate electricity for the house. Mr. de Bertodano died in 1921 and the property was sold two years later to Philip (later Sir Philip) Hunloke. Hunloke was King George V's yachtsman who moved to Malmesbury to hunt with the Beaufort.

Towards the end of August 1939 Mr. M.I. Lipman, head of the Electrical Appliances

The house during Sir Philip Hunloke's ownership. After 1940 an ugly brick building was joined to the front and the only part still visible was in the centre where a small 'courtyard' was made.

Division of E.K. Cole Ltd., was instructed by the RAF to establish a 'shadow' factory capable of producing radio equipment within a radius of 100 miles to the west of London. Eric Kirkham Cole had started making radio sets in 1924. As the business expanded it moved to a large factory in Southend-on-Sea in 1930. After searching Oxfordshire and South Gloucestershire Mr. Lipman ended up in Malmesbury and the day before war was declared bought Cowbridge House for £6,500 from Sir Philip. By Christmas Mr. Lipman had turned the house into a workshop and 20 or so workers were assembling VHF radios. Unfortunately from the start there was much ill feeling between the locals and the newcomers. Many of the young women recruited had previously been in service with the gentry. The Old Bell had a sign saying, "Employees of Messrs. E.K. Cole are not welcome in this bar". A mother with a daughter aged 17 hoped that the daughter would not be paid the minimum wage of £1 per week, as she had only been paid 10s. whilst in service in a local country house. Another young woman attracted by the higher wage was Phyllis Pike (soon to be married to George Elms who had only asked her father for permission to park his bike outside their house!). She earned £1 2s. 6d. per week winding coils and was so good at it she was often the winner of production bonuses.

The summer of 1940 saw the start of radio-location (radar) set production. Robert Watson-Watt had first demonstrated radar in 1936 when his apparatus detected a formation of planes 50 miles away. The Western Development Unit (WDU), which was established in J.E. Ponting's premises in Malmesbury's High Street, solved many of the problems of turning designs into workable sets. Some employees were brought from the parent factory in Southend but as production built up there was a shortage of labour. Other workers, many of them conscripted women, had to be brought in. About 200 women transferred from the Silk Mill when the Ministry of Supply closed that in 1941. With so many women on the staff a day nursery was set up in Swindon Road. Living accommodation had to be provided and the Priory, Halcombe House (off Foxley Road), Rodbourne House and many other properties in nearby villages were rented. In 1942 twelve prefabricated houses were erected for workers north of Cowbridge House in what would become Cowbridge Crescent. These were added to at a later date. After the war they were given to the Borough Council on the understanding that Ekco employees would have the chance of first refusal on them. Even into the 1960s there were complaints of 'queue jumping' by Ekco employees over other council tenants as 41 of the 240 council houses were covered by this agreement.

There was a strong sports and social club. Dances were held in the canteen on Saturday nights and a Ministry of Supply lorry was used to collect some of the women from the hostel in Rodbourne. On one trip, Police Inspector Edwards stopped the lorry and although he saw all the correspondence with the Ministry of Aircraft Production authorising this use, a summons was issued for Mr. Lipman to appear before the town's magistrates. The charge was using official petrol for civilian purposes. He was told by his Ministry not to worry about it but the hearing date arrived and he felt it prudent to attend

A number of Ekco electric fires that were made in the 1960s.

the court. It had not been sorted out so he asked for the case to be adjourned. The magistrate would only allow him until that afternoon so he arranged for a solicitor to be collected from Swindon who was then granted a seven day adjournment! At the following week's hearing the Ministry of Fuel's counsel asked leave to withdraw the charge. However the magistrate would have none of it and pronounced that Mr. Lipman was "guilty but discharged"! During the 1950s & 60s the Social Club provided an annual treat for the children of Malmesbury, the Christmas Party. This was held in the house and comprised entertainment including cartoon films, games and much food. The whole outing including the coach travel each way, being split into groups and the precise timetable was an exciting highlight of the year.

Ekco produced Air Interception radars for the RAF, Air to Surface Vessel sets for the Fleet Air Arm, amending these for installation in ships for the Royal Navy (and stopping the 100 valves jumping out of their sockets when guns were fired) and Search Light Control sets for the Army. At the end of the war many of the staff were made redundant, WDU went back to Southend and the factory took on other work, although radar production continued until the mid 1960s. Military

Once the house is demolished it will be very difficult to interpret this photo. This was a subsidiary entrance in the 1960s but is the main entrance now. The building on the left has been replaced by an office block, the 1940 building attached to the house is next and a glimpse of the house can be seen beyond it. The mill is obscured by another brick building which disappeared long ago.

radios (88 sets) were made and an association with Aldermaston Atomic Energy Establishment began which led to radiation monitoring equipment being produced. This was calibrated by placing a piece of radioactive material on a wooden rule and no doubt these workers received considerable exposure. Car radios, tape recorders and radiograms were added to the range of products. 1960 saw Ekco being taken over by Pye Ltd. In 1961 the Heating Appliance Division moved to Malmesbury from Southend. As a result the premises had to be extended in 1963 and again the next year at a cost of £70,000. Electric fires, Thermotube (horticultural heating in 2" steel or aluminium tubes ranging from 1' to 16' in length), night storage radiators and finally gas heaters were also produced at this time. Every day a lorry would take products to the London depot which was under the seats at Wembley Stadium! From 1969 the factory no longer traded using the Ekco name but under the TV Manufacturing Ltd. banner. However this was short-lived and the company became Pye TMC Ltd.

This name change also heralded a complete change of product. The factory now produced telephones and telephone exchange equipment. The research and development department was relocated from Dulwich which resulted in half of the building in front of

Equipment for telephone exchanges being built during the 1970s. The young lady in the centre is Sue Webb, now Deputy Town Clerk.

A 1980s aerial view of the site. The industrial workshops are to the right and Cowbridge Crescent to the left.

Cowbridge House being demolished and a modern one put up in 1975. The mid 1970s were a difficult time with 115 out of 400 workers made redundant in 1976. This was despite the arrival of the Company's head office early that year. The following year another 110 were made redundant. In 1980 Philips Telecommunications UK Ltd. took over. From then onwards the main activity was research and development of telephone equipment. From 1982 AT & T, an American telephone conglomerate joined Philips in a joint venture and in that year another modern building was put on the east of the site. However in 1986 Philips sold out their interest and AT & T became the sole owner. In the mid 1990s AT & T were finding it difficult to both operate telephone networks as well as supply equipment to competitors. They split off their manufacturing arm to form a new company, Lucent Technologies. This firm employed here some 650 staff researching and developing transmission and switching equipment for both mobile and fixed line telephone networks. Unfortunately following the collapse of the technology boom they announced the closure of this site and vacated it in September 2002.

Minton Group intend to develop the site and the only buildings to be retained are an office block to the left of the entrance and the old mill. Most of the site will be used for live/work units.

Bibliography

Ackerman, J.Y., *Malmesbury Abbey and Braden Forest* (1857) (Reprint)
Allnatt, Graham and Tomlinson, Barry, *Man in Malmesbury* (1973)
Badeni, June, *Wiltshire Forefathers* (1960)
Badeni, June, *Past People in Wiltshire and Gloucestershire* (1992)
Barnes, Dorothy, *The Archive Photographs Series: Malmesbury* (1995)
Bird, James T., *The History of the Town of Malmesbury* (1876)
Bishop, P.M., *Looking Back* (1993)
Blanchard, Joan, *Malmesbury Lace* (1990)
Bowen, John, *The Story of Malmesbury Part 1* (2000)
Box, Donald, *The Old Corporation of Malmesbury*
Bradbury, Jim, *Stephen and Matilda the Civil War of 1139-53* (1996)
Browning, Bob and Langtree, Mike, *Burton Hill House School, The first 50 years* (1997)
Chandler, John, *A Sense of Belonging* (1998)
Cobbett, William, *Rural Rides Volume Two* (1967)
Critchlow, David, *Malmesbury Beyond 2000* (1990)
Crittall, Elizabeth (ed.), *The Victoria History of Wiltshire Volume IV* (1963)
Crowley, A.D. (ed.), *The Victoria History of Wiltshire Volume XIV* (1991)
Dyson, James, *Against the odds* (1997)
Fenton, Mike, *The Malmesbury Branch* (1990)
Freeman, Jane and Watkin, Aelred, *A History of Malmesbury* (1999)
Graham, Henry, *The Annals of the Yeomanry Cavalry of Wiltshire* (1886)
Green, Walford D., *Malmesbury and its Traditions* (1935)
Hill, Paul, *Age of Athelstan* (2004)
Hobbs, Portia, *Walter Powell M.P. Balloonist* (1985)
Hodge, Dr. Bernulf, *A History of Malmesbury* (1990)
Home, Gordon and Foord, Edward, *Bristol, Bath & Malmesbury* (1925)
Hudson, Kenneth, *The Man who made Linolite* (1971)
Hudson, Stan, *A Hill Top Town* (1977)
James, M.R., *Two Ancient English Scholars St Aldhelm and William of Malmesbury* (1931)
Jefferies, Richard, *Return to Jefferies' Land* (1985)
Jenkins, G.L., *Nonconformity in Malmesbury* (1895) (Reprint)
Kelly's Directory of Wiltshire 1875-1939
List of Buildings of Special or Historic Interest, Malmesbury Area (1980)
List of Buildings of Special or Historic Interest, Malmesbury (1980)
Luce, Maj. Gen. Sir Richard, *The History of the Abbey and Town of Malmesbury* (1979)
Mackay, Maj. E.A., *The History of the Wiltshire Home Guard* (1946)
Malmesbury Civic Trust, *Twelve Centuries of Malmesbury* (1980)
Malmesbury Town Council, *The Picture Book of Malmesbury* (2001)
Mason, Kate, *Charlton Park* (1996)
Moffat, Rev. J.M., *The History of the Town of Malmesbury* (1805)
Morris, John (ed.), *Domesday Book Wiltshire* (1979)
Osborn, J. Lee, *Malmesbury* (1919)
Perkins, Rev. T., *Bath Abbey, Malmesbury Abbey, St Laurence Bradford-upon-Avon* (1901)
Pevsner, Nikolaus and Cherry, Bridget, *The Buildings of England Wiltshire* (1975)
Pigot and Company's National and Commercial Directory 1842-1844
Post Office Directory of Wiltshire 1848-1867
Powell, Anthony, *John Aubrey and his friends* (1963)

Powell, Hudson John, *Poole's Myriorama* (2002)
Preest, David, *William of Malmesbury, The Deeds of the Bishops of England* (2002)
Prince, Roberta, *Malmesbury Photographic Memories* (2004)
Pugh, R.B. and Crittall, Elizabeth (ed.), *The Victoria History of Wiltshire Volume III* (1956)
Pugh, R.B. and Crittall, Elizabeth (ed.), *The Victoria History of Wiltshire Volume V* (1957)
Punter, Vera, *Whitsunday's Child* (1993)
Ramsay, G.D., *The Wiltshire Woollen Industry in the Sixteenth and Seventeenth Centuries* (1943)
Riddick, J, *Year Book with Directory of Malmesbury 1930-1939*
Riddick, N., *History of Malmesbury* (1914)
Roger, Kenneth H., *Wiltshire and Somerset Woollen Mills* (1976)
Roger, Kenneth H., *Warp and Weft* (1986)
Roger, Kenneth H. (ed.), *Early Trade Directories of Wiltshire* (1992)
Sample, Paul, *The Oldest and the Best* (1989)
Salt, J.H., *Religious Conflicts in Elementary Schooling* (1982)
Slater's National and Commercial Directory1852-3
Smith, M.Q. and Wood, Rita, *The Sculptures of the South Porch of Malmesbury Abbey* (2002)
Stratford, J., *Wiltshire and its Worthies* (1882)
The North Wilts and District Directory for 1917-1920
The Swindon and District Directory for 1928-1939
Thomson, Rodney M., *William of Malmesbury* (1987)
Thorpe, Peter, *Moonraker Firemen (of the past) Wiltshire* (1979)
Tilney, R.D., *The Second World War Memorial, Malmesbury Wiltshire* (1999)
Tonks, Rev. William C., *Victory in the Villages* (1907) (Reprint)
Vernon, Charles, *Malmesbury Riverwalk* (2004)
Vernon, Charles, *Malmesbury Then and Now* (1999)
Weyman, Stanley, *Chippinge* (1906)
Wiltshire Archaeological and Natural History Magazine (Various)
Winch, T.B.C., *Malmesbury Abbey Royal Coat of Arms*
Woosnam, M., *Eilmer 11th Century Monk of Malmesbury* (1986)
1100th Anniversary Committee, *Malmesbury 1100 years a Borough* (1980)

Index